The Harvest of the Spirit

The
Harvest
of the Spirit

Landrum P. Leavell

BROADMAN PRESS
Nashville, Tennessee

4219-37
ISBN: 0-8054-1937-3

Dewey Decimal Classification: 227.4
Subject Headings: BIBLE N.T. GALATIANS 5:22 // HOLY SPIRIT
Library of Congress Catalog Card Number: 76-4373
Printed in the United States of America

This Book Is Dedicated
in deep gratitude to my alma mater

The New Orleans Baptist Theological Seminary

beloved school of Providence and prayer,
including faculty, administration, staff
and students, past and present,
living and dead.

Foreword

When the invitation came a number of years ago from Broadman to submit a manuscript of sermonic material on the three Johannine epistles, I responded by saying that I could do this only if the editors would be able to use the material which I would preach on the subject. This has been true of each subsequent volume, culminating with this present work. The focus of my life and calling, the preaching ministry, has become the source and substance of these books.

There has been a tremendous wave of interest in the doctrine of the Holy Spirit during recent years. Numerous books have been published on this vital subject. I do not know of any other entire volume devoted to Paul's inspired words in Galatians 5:22-23. Perhaps this one will help to fill the gap. Possibly others might be motivated to contribute to the understanding of these inspired and challenging words.

It is humanly impossible to recall and name all those persons and sources to whom I am indebted for help, encouragement, and insights included in this material. Suffice it to say that I owe a great debt to numbers of persons, and my heart is truly grateful for assistance in my spiritual pilgrimage.

This series of sermons was first preached under the title, "Christ in You," from the pulpit of First Baptist Church, Wichita Falls, Texas. It is my conviction that these nine characteristics will mark the life of a person in whom Jesus Christ is living as Lord. It is my prayer that something found here will assist you in spiritual growth until the day when "we shall be like him, for we shall see him as he is."

LANDRUM P. LEAVELL

CONTENTS

1.
Christ in You:
Love

The primary meaning of the Greek word *karpos* is harvest. This is the word found in Galatians 5:22, translated "fruit" in the King James. I prefer the word *harvest*. There are some other meanings given to this word: work, deed, act, and you could substitute any one of these words for the word *fruit* here and come up with a little different slant on what Paul was saying. I think the word *harvest* sums up the spirit of Paul far more adequately than the word *fruit*.

Paul wrote the harvest of the Holy Spirit is love. Many of us feel that the most beautiful time of the year, though we love all the seasons, is the fall of the year. Fall is always associated with harvest. It's in the fall of the year that the farmer is able to reap what he has sown. The rewards of man's labor and the riches of God's goodness are abundantly evident in the harvest time. What is true in the natural life is also true in the spiritual life.

In our text we find the harvest of the Christ-dominated life. This is what results when Christ is in you, or as Paul put it in another place, "Christ in you, the hope of glory." When Christ resides in us, the harvest of his presence is love.

Let's look at that first fruit of the harvest. In the Greek text it is the word *agape*. That's an interesting word, for it has no known historical antecedent prior to the New Testament. The Greeks had other words for love. They had the word *eros,* which is the sensual, fleshly love. They had the word *philos* which referred to the love one has for his brother, his own blood kin, or those who are his spiritual kinsmen. But the New Testament writers knew there was no word in the language that pictured the kind of love that God revealed in Jesus. And so the Greek word *agape* appears for the first time in the New Testament era. It's a new word, a different word, and describes something that man had never envisioned or tried to describe prior to this time. This *agape* love is the Calvary kind of love. It's the kind revealed in the sacrifice and suffering of the Lord Jesus Christ. Now when Jesus Christ comes into our lives, that's the kind of love which comes in, a sacrificing, self-denying kind of love.

We must admit the indictment of a question Jesus posed in the New Testament. He asked, "If ye love them which love you, what reward have ye?" (Matt. 5:46). That proposition is simply this: It's not hard to love those who love us, and if we only love those who love us, what have we done? The implication is you haven't done anything. It's easy to love those who love you. It's easy to love those of your own social-economic stratum. It's easy to love those whose skin is the same color as your own, but if those are the only people you love, what have you done? You haven't done anything! The Calvary kind of love is the love that enables us to love those who hate us, who would spit in our faces, who would mock us, who would curse us, and who would even hurl a spear into our flesh. That's the *agape* kind of love. And that's the kind of love that comes in when Christ comes in.

If you are a true believer, Christ lives in your heart. If

Christ lives there, this kind of love lives there; so my suggestion is very simple. I am suggesting that Christ in you means
love in you. Not the *eros* kind of love, not the *philos* kind
of love, but the *agape* kind of love. This kind was revealed
in that central cross among the three crosses on Calvary's
brow. Let me further suggest that this love is powerful,
productive and pervasive. It's—

Powerful.

I say that because there is an antidote for the misery of
meaninglessness that has afflicted our generation. There is
a powerful cure. That antidote is this love, a strange new
power that surges through life like streams in a desert. Life
does not remain flat, insipid, and tasteless. Depth, desire,
and delight come on like waves of the ocean when Christ
lives in us. The Holy Spirit who imparts this life makes
us know we cannot save ourselves; then he reveals to us
the fact that we cannot keep ourselves saved. You can't do
either, nor can I. The Holy Spirit is powerful to do both,
effecting God's work in the life of a human being, He is
powerful to save and powerful to keep. All of our goodness
or righteousness is impotent, but he's powerful.

He's the One who introduces this love into the life of
a believer. We possess him from the very instant of repentance and faith. But the fact is he does not possess us until
we surrender our wills to him.

Texas Electric has unbelievable energy resources. Yet all
the fantastic energy resources of Texas Electric are of absolutely no value in our building until the switch is thrown.
We can only utilize that power when, by an act of will,
we throw a switch. Then electricity becomes operative and
light becomes helpful. The switch has to be thrown. Regard-

less of the amount of reserve, regardless of the ability of that organization to develop this energy, it is of no value to you or me until we put it to use by an act of will. This is also true of the love of God. It is of no value to a human being until we flip the switch. The energy is there but man determines whether or not he will utilize that energy.

The love of God is powerless until we throw the switch of self-denial and self-surrender. As long as we remain stubborn, coldhearted, and hardheaded the power of God available to us in indescribable quantity is of absolutely no value. If we throw the switch, it means we relinquish the hold we have on our lives. It means we sever our moorings and set ourselves adrift in the love and purpose of God. This is embodied in the words of a song that says, "I'll go where You want me to go, dear Lord, O'er mountain or plain or sea; I'll say what You want me to say, dear Lord, I'll be what You want me to be." Now this isn't a passing fancy. This is a studied commitment in which we yield ourselves to him and his directing power.

When he takes over, there's a new life, a new fire, a new power, and we become alive for the first time. This is life in the power of God. When that takes place, Paul stated the characteristics that come as a result: "Love bears all things, believes all things, hopes all things, endures all things, love never ends." How many there are who have sat in my office and asked, "How much do I have to put up with? How long do I have to allow this to continue? There is a breaking point." That may be true from the human standpoint, but from the point of view of the love of God, love bears all things, believes all things, hopes all things, and endures all things. Love never fails. Now if what you call love fails, that's proof it is not the Christ kind of love. It's not the love produced in the harvest of the Holy Spirit, for the harvest of the Spirit includes *agape* kind of love. That's what Paul described in 1 Corinthians 13. That love gives victory over hate, selfishness, discord, jealousy, wrath, envy, and anger. This is the most powerful force in the world. When Christ lives in us, that power is operative through us. Not only is it powerful; his love is also—

Productive.

Love is beautiful on the inside and on the outside. It's beautiful to possess, but it's likewise marvelous to behold. If that kind of love marks your life, your life becomes magnetic and attractive and others will see Christ living in you.

Paul, in 1 Corinthians 13, said, "Love is patient and kind." You know, patience and kindness are twins. They walk in cadence one with the other. Patience is passive. It can put up with infinite injury and never reach the breaking point. What a transformation would come in our home relationships if our lives were marked by this kind of love. Love is patient and kind. It can suffer and suffer and suffer some more and never break. That's the kind of love Christ revealed. That's the kind of love he introduced to us when he came into our lives. Patience can put up with so much, and kindness can put out so much. Kindness never encountered a person it could not love.

Love does not produce jealousy or boasting, Paul wrote. In the King James translation of 1 Corinthians 13 we find the words "envieth not." This is jealousy and boasting, and actually they are twins also. These twins are not produced by love. Jealousy and boasting are evidences of an unregenerate life, or at least a life in which the love of God has not been shed abroad. Jealousy is the sin of the "have nots."

Jealousy sees another person who possesses more. Boasting, on the other hand, is the sin of the "haves." It's the know-it-all, do-it-all, have-it-all sort of attitude that's so utterly repugnant in the life of a human being. If jealousy sees someone else with position, personality, ability, with a reputation or material possessions beyond its own, then things begin to warm up. The derivation of the word *jealousy* in the Greek is fascinating. It comes from the Greek word *zeo*, and it actually means to boil or to be hot. Can you discern this in your own life? Jealous people get warm, then they simmer, and then come to a boil. Sometimes they even reach a percolating point!

But boasting is no better. It brags and blows its horn and repulses other people. These are not marks of the harvest of the Spirit. Patience and kindness are.

Love does not produce arrogance or rudeness. Again the King James Version has it, "vaunteth not itself, is not puffed up." I think Paul is trying to say that love does not strut around like a peacock, nor does it paw the ground and snort through its nostrils like a mad bull. When those characteristics are evident, love is not present. Love does not produce arrogance or rudeness. These two are twins. You'd better believe it's dangerous to get in their way. If you happen to be in the path of arrogance or rudeness, you're in for a rough time.

By contrast, a life lived in Christ possesses a wonderful attitude. In Christ all is well, for love abides and love says, "If you don't do it my way, I'll do it your way." Love does not insist on its own way.

Remember Jesus in the garden of Gethsemane. Did he say, "Father, I've got a better idea. This is my conviction, Father. This is the way it must be done"? Love is not the "rule or ruin" spirit. Love does not insist on having its own way. Love prefers the long road with companions and friends to walking alone on a shorter road in the loneliness of dejection and despair.

Paul stated, "Love is not irritable or resentful." What a transformation there would be in the homes of America if love were present. I'm talking about the Christ kind of love. Love is not touchy; love doesn't get sore; love doesn't pout and clam up; love doesn't throw a fit; love doesn't carry a chip on its shoulder.

I read avidly Ann Landers and Dear Abby. There's some great advice in those two columns, and if you don't read them you ought to start. Just recently one of those sisters, and I understand they are blood sisters, suggested to a person who was looking for a fight, carrying a chip on his shoulder, that the presence of a chip on one's shoulder is an indication there is wood up above! Now I don't think you can beat that truth!

Love keeps no books on unkind deeds and unkind words. Love doesn't remember that hurt which was inflicted last month or last year or five years ago. Love doesn't remember that sin when someone stumbled back in the past. Love does not hold other people accountable for past sins which God has forgiven. That's not the way of love. Love knows that brooding embitters the soul. Love does not rejoice in evil but rejoices in good. I think we could probably sum it up this way: love's vote can be counted before the election because love is always on the right side. The fruit of the Spirit, the harvest of the Spirit, is love. This is powerful and it's productive. It produces a different attitude, a different spirit, a different nature, and a new way of life. There's one other word. This love is also—

Pervasive.

Why is it, you ask, that some people who have earnestly trusted Christ have never experienced the harvest of the Spirit? Why is it that some people you and I know, who have been Christians for years on end, still give no evidence of love in their lives? I believe the only answer is they have never yet applied the principles of the Christian faith. Many of them are still trying in their own strength and they're failing.

Sometimes these come in a public rededication of their lives. Then a few days or a few weeks or months after the decision, they lapse into their old ways. What happens? They tried to do it themselves and they failed. I can think of no better way than to cast our burden upon the Lord, for there is no other successful way.

Begin your day with 1 John 1:9, "If we confess our sins, he is faithful and just to forgive us our sins, and to cleanse us from all unrighteousness." What's our obligation? To confess our sins. What's his obligation? To be faithful and just to forgive us our sins.

Now why is it necessary for you to confess your sins to Christ? The reason is, he is the One against whom we have sinned. That burning hatred and animosity and jealousy which you hold in your heart is not against another individual, it is sin against Jesus Christ that allows continuing hatred, animosity, and jealousy in the life of a believer. Why is this a sin against Christ, you ask? It's because the lost person and the worldly church member see something in you that is utterly false. The lost person sees you as you give an untrue picture of what Christ does in the heart of a believer. This makes the lost world mock and sneer and jeer at Jesus Christ. When you sin, your sin may have a horizontal direction, but its primary thrust is vertical, for you have sinned against Christ. When the lost person sees unregenerate characteristics in you or me, that lost person thinks Christ is powerless.

The youth of this day have learned well the lesson of criticism. Some of the young people in America are vehement in their denunciation of the older generation's hypocrisy. Our hypocrisy needs condemnation, but so also does their sanctimonious attitude on Sunday and around the church, when they go home and treat their parents like dogs. Yes, you have a right to be critical of the older generation, but there comes a time when you've got to have enough courage to face up to your own ego and the stink of sin in your own life. Some young people make their home a living hell, and they're not sinning just against their parents, they're sinning against the Lord Jesus Christ. Young people, you glory in your flesh, you're proud of your self-righteousness; but if Christ lives in you, you'll treat your parents with respect as the New Testament requires of a Christian. Your ugliness, your bitterness, your unkindness toward your family and your acquaintances is a mark of sin in your flesh.

It may well be that my generation is guilty of prejudice, but we're trying to fight it. I'll tell you what: the most prejudiced group in America today is probably those high-school-aged girls who pick and choose their friends and exclude all others. If you want to know what bitterness, littleness, and meanness is all about, you'll see it in the way they treat one another. Yes, you have a right to criticize the older generation, but you do not have the right to be arrogant in regard to your own sin, for your sin is also a sin against Jesus Christ. You can be just as prejudiced toward another girl in your own peer group as the older generation may have been prejudiced toward people whose skin is a different color. Amen?

If Christ lives in you, love will abide in your life. You must expand your capacity for gratitude and thankfulness. Every blessing that comes to you which you take for granted, for which you do not express thanks, causes you to lose your capacity to say thank-you. How seldom does a parent hear from a child in the home a sincere, heartfelt thank-you! How seldom are those two little words articulated by the younger generation! When you take for granted everything your parents have done for you, you're shriveling your own soul.

You know, I thank God for a group of people who are letter writers. They sit down and write letters to say thank-you. Most of the time the letters aren't deserved; most of the time it's for something that hardly demands any notice; but isn't it a joy to find gratitude and thankfulness in the life of a human being? That characteristic ought to mark the life of every person who lives in Christ Jesus. When we miss the opportunity to express our love and thanks-giving, we lose that capacity. It may be that the capacity you have for thanksgiving has been shrunk to the size of a teaspoon. My friend, you have the ability to expand it to the size of a tablespoon, and then by expressing thanks sincerely, openly, genuinely, you can expand that capacity to the size of a number three washtub! That's the sort of capacity that we ought to have when Christ is in us and we're producing the harvest of the Spirit, which is love.

Now lust may be felt suddenly, but love takes time. You don't plant seed with one hand and gather the harvest with the other hand. This is true in the spiritual life also. God plants the seed but the fruit does not come up instantly.

We have to cultivate it. We have to work at it. We have to stay busy doing the things that are necessary. But the presence of love in our lives is the ultimate, irrefutable proof that Christ is in our lives.

Celsus, who was the critic of early Christians, once said, "These Christians love each other even before they are acquainted." He thought that was humorous. He said it as a slur, but what a wonderful tribute! These Christians love each other even before they are acquainted. Jesus said: "By this shall all men know that ye are my disciples, if ye have love one to another" (John 13:35). That's the normal harvest of the Spirit of God. Is that harvest present in your life?

2.
Christ in You:
Joy

Paul used a singular here when he wrote the *fruit* or the *harvest* of the Holy Spirit. Most of us, in view of the wide and wonderful variety of these spiritual graces, would have thought he used the plural, the *fruits* or the *harvests* of the Holy Spirit. The emphasis seems to be upon the fact that all that's mentioned in verses 22 and 23 constitutes one fruit. This is what the Holy Spirit does when he dwells in the life of a believer. It's well said that "joy dwells in the house of love nor elsewhere will she tarry." Joy is the zest of life. When the springs of joy go dry, the spirit of a man loses its vitality and magnetism like a flower uprooted from the soil.

This joy can be illustrated in a number of ways. I think, for instance, of the unfeigned, simple laughter of a little child. It's sheer delight to hear a baby laugh. This is an illustration of joy. In the laughter of a baby there's no bitterness, no sarcasm, no criticism, nor any "I told you so" attitude. You can hear laughter today as bitter as the dregs of gall, but the laughter of a little child is undiluted joy.

There is another illustration of joy that I observe from time to time, and that's the benign, quiet smile of an aged person who has grown old with all grace and in the Spirit of Jesus Christ. Have you observed this? A person who is

not trying to prove a point, an individual who is not trying
to elbow anyone else out of the way, who's not trying to
make a second million or a third million, but who has
reached the point of sweet repose in life and can smile
without any bitterness whatever. That's the kind of joy I
believe the Holy Spirit plants in the heart of a believer.
I think in the first place we understand joy as—

Devotion.

There won't be any real joy without this quality. These
nine virtues enumerated in our text may seem to have been
written without any semblance of order. They may just seem
to have been shuffled together and cast out, so to speak.
Yet as we examine them carefully we can determine a signif-
icant progression from one to another.

The first named is the basis, the foundation upon which
all else is built. The fruit or the harvest of the Spirit is love.
That's first. You don't build a superstructure until the foundation has been laid. The foundation for all of these virtues
is the love of God which has been shed abroad richly in
our hearts through the grace of the Lord Jesus Christ.

In these verses we have a trio of triads. There are three
sets of characteristics containing three virtues each. The first
three are love, joy, and peace. These are personal possessions
in the heart of a believer. These have to do with me. They
have to do with you as an individual: love, joy, peace.

The next three: longsuffering, gentleness, and goodness
are dispositions I reveal toward my fellowman. I'm longsuffering in relation to another person. I'm gentle in relation
to other people. I'm good in relation to other human beings.

But then the third group of three, faith, meekness (and
this probably is better translated humility), and temperance

are attitudes that have special reference to my relationship with God. And so the harvest of the Holy Spirit concerns me, my neighbor, and my Lord. When we're in right relationship with him, these are the natural products of that relationship. He's the One who guarantees the harvest, and it comes as a result of his indwelling presence in our lives.

It's little wonder that love is the foundation upon which all the others are built. It is love that makes us capable of shame and pain. But it is also love that makes us capable of triumph and delight. There's no sorrow in life like the sorrow of Christ rejected. There is no joy in life compared to the joy of Christ accepted, risen, and reigning in the life of the believer.

This joy is devotion in that it requires a commitment to something beyond ourselves. We all become devoted to something or someone else. That's a secret many people have never found. That's the key human beings by the thousands have never discovered.

The self-centered life is never happy. Find a self-centered individual and you'll find one who is restless, uneasy, critical, always on the move and can never relax and never seems to discern the true joys life has to offer. Those who live for self alone never know the indescribable joys that come through service to one's fellowman.

You know, there's a joy in owning a new automobile. I must confess to you I like the smell of a new car. It just does something for me. Now there are some people whom that does not turn on. I know; I live with one. It just doesn't mean one thing to her. But I like the smell of a new car. When you buy a new car and get that burst of joy which comes as you drive it home, park it, shut the door, step back, and look at it, and then get back into it and smell it again, you know that smell eventually will wear off. Then the paint gets cracked. You come down to the parking lot of the First Baptist Church and some inconsiderate dolt opens his car door and knocks the paint off the side. Maybe some member of the family dents the fender. What happens? The joy is soon gone because it was a temporal joy.

There's a joy that comes in owning a new home, but then come the ravages of time. The paint begins to crack and peel and the colors fade. The new is gone and after a period of years the new is lost and the original joy has gone with it. But that is temporal joy. It's the joy we get over possessions. It's not the real joy that comes as the harvest of the Holy Spirit. Real joy, heartfelt joy, is not found in great causes or great possessions or in other people. The greatest joy of all is found in the Lord when we've made things right with him and have done our utmost to fulfill his calling. That's where real joy comes. It's described in various ways, but one passage calls it "the peace of God that passeth all understanding." That kind of joy can't be bought with the purchase of a new car, or a new home, or acquiring any one of a thousand possessions this world offers.

The Lord created us and gave us the capacity of fulfilling our joy in him. Any other joy therefore will be fleeting. Any other joy will soon be gone. It's only in him that we find lasting joy. So joy is found in devotion. It's devotion to someone else, and that someone is Jesus Christ. When this alignment is correct vertically, our horizontal alignment with our fellowman will be proper. But the first one is the vertical one. We're in right relationship with him, so then our joy is full. Now recall that this joy requires—

Depletion.

I mean a depletion of all worldly, material resources upon which we have depended to bring us joy. As long as we're depending upon things, we'll never know the joy that comes as the result of the presence of the Holy Spirit. It is not dependent upon the size of our savings account, the number of automobiles in the driveway or the garage, or the amount of shares of blue chip securities contained in the portfolio. This joy is experienced when we are depleted of material resources and can say with the songwriter, "Nothing in my hand I bring, simply to Thy cross I cling." As long as we're clinging to these material resources, real joy will elude us.

In Acts 16, Paul and Silas were socially and financially depleted. They were social outcasts, and had received the ultimate disgrace. They had been thrown in jail for having preached the gospel which they believed so strongly. Can you think of any conditions which might bring misery and woe more quickly than being in a cold, dark, dank dungeon? It may have had standing water on the floor, and if so there was mud in which they stood or sat. That was the sort of situation which existed. Some of us have visited the Mamertine Prison in Rome where Paul was held for possibly two years. There was no concrete there. There were no sanitary facilities. It was just a dungeon, a hole in the ground. Here were Paul and Silas in a place like that. Yet their cup of joy was so full that revival broke out in that dungeon.

This leads us to understand that the depth of our joy is in direct proportion to our renunciation of worldly things. As long as we're holding on to the things the world offers, our joy will not be full. When outward circumstances are demanded to control the inner life, there's no real joy. When you've got to have a certain priced house or a certain priced car, or you must have other things this world offers to be happy, then you're really not happy! You are of all men most miserable, for you become anxious lest you lose these things and you know that what little joy you have will be gone when they go. That's why I say that joy requires depletion. We have to be depleted of our dependence upon things this world has to offer.

It was said of Jesus, "For the joy that was set before him endured the cross, despising the shame." Can you imagine? Was there joy in looking forward to the cross, enduring the agony of it, and despising the shame of it? Yes, that's exactly what the New Testament says! "For the joy that was set before him." It was a joy that came not because of outward circumstances, for they were the most horrible imaginable. It was joy that came through the knowledge that this was what God had sent him into the world to do. That's why our Lord could say, "For this cause came I into the world." That's where his joy was found. That's where you and I find joy. Not in building up a fortune and worldly things, but in building up our faith in the resources of God who has promised to supply all our need.

Philip Bliss wrote, " 'Man of sorrows!' what a name/For the Son of God who came/Ruined sinners to reclaim!/Hallelujah, what a Saviour!"/Joy is found when we commit ourselves totally to him. We see this joy as devotion, in depletion, and also we must know it as a—

Desire.

The harvest of the Holy Spirit described in our text describes all of the relationships of life. The suggestion is that a life under the power and control of the Holy Spirit is one of full-orbed beauty. The stress here is upon what we are, and what we are always determines the value of what we do. So many people never get this straight. Many never understand this. That is why we get confused about salvation by works. That's why so many people ascribe a certain goodness to folks who are outside the kingdom of God. "Oh, he's a good man! I know he wasn't a church man, or he didn't go to church, or he's not a professing Christian, but he's a good man." The point is, what we *are* determines the value of what we *do*. If we are self-centered, if we're egotistical, if we're still paying homage to self, no matter how many poor people we might help in a time of trouble, no matter how many worthy philanthropic deeds we may perform, the credit for those belongs to the individual who is seeing to it that what he does is known! When we *are* something on the inside, when we are fully Christ's, then everything we do is going to be done for Christ. What we are on the inside determines the value of what we do. So many have never perceived that spiritual truth.

If these qualities of the Spirit constitute a harvest, let's keep in mind that this harvest comes by growth and not by self-effort. A lot of you were raised on the farm. After you planted corn, did you go out every day and help it grow? Did you pat it, encourage it, and say, "Come on up now, come on, let's go." No, you planted the seed and then had to wait. You had to wait on the rain, and on the elements. Maybe you got out there once in a while and did a little plowing or running around the rows to try to keep the weeds out, but you did not do a thing to insure the growth of that seed after it was planted. You just had to wait.

This is precisely true in the life of a believer. The harvest of the Holy Spirit takes time. It requires thàt the time elapsing be spent in spiritual pursuits that will create a climate

conducive to growth. I think this is the reason so many
Christians are unhappy, or at least so many church members.
This is the reason why so many church members never have
caught fire. The seed has been planted, but there is no
climate for growth. The climate for growth requires prayer,
Bible study, discipline, faithfulness, and regularity. If our
lives are marked by failure and woeful inconsistency, if we
nevertheless are trying to create the climate in which the
harvest can come, then we may know the Holy Spirit one
day will produce these fruits. I don't think anybody here
would say, "I'm an evidence of these fruits or harvest of
the Holy Spirit." But I'll tell you one thing: I do possess
in my soul the hope that God will produce these in me and
as much as in me lies, I'm going to try to provide the climate
that will make it conducive for the seed the Holy Spirit
drops to grow in my heart and life.

Now that requires a desire. It's a desire on your part and
mine to go where he wants us to go, to be what he wants
us to be, to do what he wants us to do, and to say what
he wants us to say. He's not going to require you to do
something and make you do it. He's going to challenge you
to do his will, and the desire is left up to you and me. We
have to have the desire to overcome negativism, pessimism.
We have to develop a desire to overcome our inertia and
lack of loyalty and unfaithfulness. We must have a desire
to rise above these things and to be more like the Master
day by day.

These things are sin since the fruit of the Spirit involves
the opposite to those things I've just mentioned. If you want
to have an interesting experience, take your Bible and read
the preceding verses of chapter 5 of the Galatian epistle.
There Paul contrasted the works of the flesh with the fruit

of the Spirit. Just study those for awhile. There is another
series of sermons that would take about six months, because
one could preach a sermon on every one of those evidences
of worldliness, the evidence of the devil in the life of a
human being.

In Ephesians 5:18 we read, "Be filled with the Spirit."
This is an interesting passage of Scripture because of the
verb form. Listen to the four different things that are true
about this verb form. "Be filled with the Spirit," First of
all it is in the imperative mode. That means it is imperative
because God commands it, and because the fullness of the
Holy Spirit is the divine enablement in the life of a Christian.
In other words, we are nothing without him. "Be filled with
the Spirit." That's imperative.

There's a second thing. The tense of this verb is present,
and that signifies continuous action. "Be ye filled with the
Spirit" again and again and again, over and over and over,
and that says the Spirit-filled life is not spasmodic but
constant. It's not one burst of speaking in an unknown tongue
and then you're through with it. It is a continuous relationship between yourself and God, and between yourself
and other people. "Be ye filled with the Spirit." Present tense.

Third, this verb is plural in number. Now that says the
filling of the Holy Spirit is not just for the preacher, or for
the deacons, or for the Sunday School teachers. This filling
is for every born-again believer in Jesus Christ. It is your
responsibility to be filled with the Spirit!

There's a fourth thing, and I tell you, I could preach a
whole sermon on this one verb. One verb, a whole sermon.
The fourth thing is it's in the passive voice in the Greek,
and that represents the subject of the verb as being inactive
and being acted upon from the outside. Now what does that

say? It says that you and I, to be filled with the Spirit, are the inactive objects. This is the work of God from the outside coming upon us. This says salvation is not of works! The filling of the Holy Spirit does not come when we do more and work faster or talk louder. It comes when we prostrate ourselves before him. When we do, this is something he does for us.

The harvest of the Holy Spirit! He plants the seed and brings it forth, but you and I have to provide the ready receptacle. The requirement for this filling is desire. God's not going to produce a harvest in you or through you against your will. You must want more than anything else to display love, joy, peace, longsuffering, meekness, temperance, goodness, faith—these things against which there is no law. You've got to want it, and when you want it, he'll take over and provide you with the seed that will bring forth this harvest.

So the question is, "Does Christ control your life?" If he does, one of the results is going to be joy—the kind of joy that's yours every day. It's not a come and go proposition, it's constant. It's daily joy, and it causes you to look forward to a new day, a new week, to new opportunities, and to doing specific tasks. It is the joy of looking forward to an opportunity to share Christ with anyone you meet anywhere you go. That's the kind of joy in you every day as the Holy Spirit controls your life.

3.
Christ in You:
Peace

In the Galatian epistle, the apostle Paul is sounding a warning that those who have been justified by faith must walk in the Spirit. Paul wrote that those justified through faith in Jesus Christ are no longer to walk after the flesh. We have not been justified by faith if we continue to walk after that which is fleshly and not spiritual. This argument has been presented in the Galatian epistle in chapters and verses preceding our text. He comes now to present two kinds of harvest.

Those who have read the fifth chapter of Galatians again and again will recall that he also lists those diabolical evils produced by a walk after the flesh: envyings, murders, drunkenness, and all those other things which are abhorrent even today. One harvest is produced when we walk in the flesh; the other harvest is inevitably produced when we walk after the Spirit.

It seems that Paul is trying to say there is a danger in confusing mere intellectual perception with the faith of the Christian gospel. Paul suggests that you can believe something with your mind which will not necessarily transform your actions.

I believe certain men were blasted off a launching pad at Cape Kennedy, and after making a turn or so around the earth in orbit, went to the moon. I believe that, but it is not experiential because I have never done that. It is intellectual perception. I believe it, but it has not affected me because I've never experienced it.

You can take that very simple illustration and apply it to the Christian gospel. This is the reasoning Paul is using. It's possible to know something with your mind and never have experienced it. Paul insists that it's impossible for a man who walks after the Spirit to produce the harvest of the flesh, and it's impossible for a man walking after the flesh to produce the harvest of the Spirit. They are two separate aeons. They are mutually exclusive.

I believe we would agree that no religion is worthy that does not make a man a better man, that does not make a son a better son, a father a better father, a mother a better mother, or a daughter a better daughter. I'm saying with Paul that your religion is vain if it has not transformed your character. What good would it be to claim the Christian faith and give no evidence of transformation? If your religion does not produce good fruit, it is not the Christian faith.

Paul has asserted this dogmatically in the Galatian letter. John the Baptist stated it without equivocation. John said that every tree that bringeth not forth good fruit, that is the harvest of the Spirit, is hewn down and cast into the fire. This is the same argument Paul is using, and it's the premise for this treatment. Christ in you will result in a harvest that includes peace: peace of heart and peace in your relationship toward other people. This is a fruit of the Spirit. It comes naturally as a result of love and joy. These are the two virtues we've considered previously, and I believe that under the inspiration of the Holy Spirit Paul wrote these in studied sequence.

The harvest of the Spirit has love as its foundation. Building upon that foundation comes joy, and then peace. These virtues have their source in God. They are sustained and maintained only by his presence and power. These are not human achievements. These are not qualities we can work for, and with our little piosities insure their presence. These are gifts of God, and they come as the result of walking in the Spirit.

There are passages that reveal these come from God. For instance, "Love is of God." The person then who does not know God does not know true love. There is a verse that states, "We rejoice in the Lord." That says joy comes from God. Throughout the New Testament we read again and again about the peace of God that keeps our minds and hearts in Christ Jesus. So love, joy, and peace are not virtues that come from human achievements. These are gifts that result from a relationship with God. If Christ is in you, peace will be in you. Now this peace has three directions, in my judgment. I'd like to suggest the direction is—

Upward.

Christian peace does not come from the absence of trouble, but rather by the presence of God. A child of God, with warfare and fighting and dissensions and turmoils and chaos all around, can nonetheless walk with unruffled ease in the midst of conflict. Like the three Hebrew children in the fiery furnace, one who has a right relationship with God in an upward dimension may possess peace. The depth of our peace will be in exact measure to the degree in which we live in and partake of the love of God. Little peace, little love; a shallow peace, a shallow relationship with God; a deep and abiding peace, a deep and abiding relationship with our Maker.

In Galatians 1:3 Paul wrote, "Grace to you and peace *from* God the Father and our Lord Jesus Christ." Do you see the connection in that sentence? "Grace to you and peace from . . ." It comes from God, our Father. Grace is the fundamental relationship, for it is by grace that we are accepted into the family of God. It is by grace that we are brought nigh unto God, and he receives us. It's by his grace our sins are forgiven. Grace is foundational, and when grace has been experienced, peace is the result.

There's no passage in Holy Writ where this sequence is reversed. There's no way biblically speaking for a person to receive peace prior to receiving grace. The One who opens for us the gates of grace is the One who opens the floodgates of peace and sheds it abroad in our hearts and lives. Grace comes first and then peace.

The Greek word for peace is the word *eirene*. It's equivalent to the Hebrew *shalom*. They both mean the same. It's the condition of well-being when God is our friend and all is well. This word has two very interesting uses in the New Testament. The Greek *eirene* refers to the tranquillity and serenity of a nation under the just and beneficent government of a good ruler. Isn't that a beautiful picture? The other meaning of this word stands for everything that contributes to man's highest and best good. That's God's peace. It comes when we know God has accepted us, not on the basis of our worthiness but our worthlessness, and that anything God wants to do for us, through us, and with us, is in our best interests. One who has that assurance possesses peace!

This peace is the harmony that reveals holiness. It is the relationship by which a man says to the world, "I am a

saint of God through my faith in the Lord Jesus." It is contrasted with discord. Find an individual in whose life there
is a civil war and you will find a person in whom the devil
is holding a jamboree. When God is present, peace is the
inevitable result. Christ in you—the result is peace. It is an
upward relationship, but it is also—

Inward.

The peace problem is solved in the substitution of reason
for force, right for might, and law for war. This product
of the presence of the Holy Spirit is a settled quiet of the
heart. It is a deep, brooding mystery that exceeds man's
ability to comprehend. We look in amazement at those who
possess it. We wonder, in the midst of the troubles and
conflicts of their lives, how they possess this kind of assurance. We can't understand it. It doesn't come by a doctor's
prescription. It can't be bought in the pharmacy in the form
of a tranquilizer. It does not find it's location in the bottom
of a bottle containing alcoholic beverage. This peace is not
a result of the ownership of certain material possessions.

We can take a gun from a drunk man, a crazy man, or
a burglar, but by the use of superior force the taking of
a gun from a drunk will not make him sober and the taking
of a gun from a crazy person will not insure sanity. The
removal of a gun from a burglar will not guarantee honesty.
The kind of peace that is produced by compulsion is but
the calm that accompanies enforced slavery. The peace of
God is not that which is guaranteed by superior might and
power, though God has that power.

The peace that God gives comes not as a result of surrender
to superior force, but as the surrender of what we are and
have. This peace belongs to those who have been justified

by faith. It is the gift of Jesus Christ, who according to the New Testament, made peace through the blood of his cross. Jesus, who made peace, offers peace to those who come on his terms. He has brought us to terms with the law of the eternal God. He has brought us to an understanding of God's will, which is over all and exceeds all.

It is because of this peace that we pass from the region of mad rebellion and revolution into the freedom of God's love and provision. After that total war we have fought with our own emotions, after the tempest and the warfare of doubt and fear, Jesus Christ our regnant King speaks his "Peace be still." When Christ, who made peace for us, imparts peace to our troubled hearts, it is then that a great calm spreads over the boisterous waters, the wind and the waves lie hushed at the feet of him who has authority over them. The demonic powers that brought this tumult into being vanishes to nothing, for Christ is Lord of all. The fruit of the presence of Jesus Christ is peace. It is revealed to the world in the witness of a Christian by that calm, unruffled brow. It is seen in a poise and even temper that reveals the presence of Christ.

Honestly now, are you satisfied with that hellish disposition? Are you content to live, not by reason, but by force, and the rage of your emotions? Do you take sadistic pleasure in keeping others in abeyance before your temper?

You may possess a temper, but my friend, do not attribute it to the presence of Christ in your life. Christ in you means peace in you. When you have made peace with God, then you come to terms with yourself. You make peace with who you are, with what you have, and with what you can contribute to the society in which you live. I have often maintained that it is an impossibility for a Christian to be gripped by an inferiority complex! To whom should a child of God ever feel inferior? When you understand this upward dimension, your relationship from God to man and from man to God, and when you've gotten that squared away through your faith in Jesus, then you can come to terms with yourself.

I am not Billy Graham. I've reached the point in my own personality growth and development where I can thank God that I am not. I can thank God that I am who I am, that he made me, that he has a place for me, and that it is a unique position that only I can fill. My talents do not compare with the talents of thousands of other ministers of the gospel. But that's not the point. The point is I must not spend my life feeling inferior to any other human. God made me, God called me, God put me where I am, and my only responsibility is to serve him in the place where he put me. Now friend, when you have that sort of assurance, you can have peace in your heart. You don't have to be continuously fighting, allowing your temper to get the best of you, keeping others in virtual slavery because of your hellish spirit. When God's peace comes, you have the joy of knowing that God has opened for you a door of service, and it is in that place that you can find joy and fulfillment.

Do we need that kind of peace today? The hate and the hell that is a part of the world in which we live is simply a revelation of the civil war taking place in the hearts of men. In some ways peace is like marriage. No marriage is successful if two people merely sign a marriage license. A successful marriage comes when two people, every day, live in the reality of their love for each other and work in cooperation to make the marriage what it ought to be. Peace is like that. Peace doesn't come when you just say with your mind, "I believe in Jesus, I believe in Christ, I accept him as my Savior." Peace comes when with the totality of your being you commit your life to him in faith and trust; when you accept what he has given you and what he expects you to do; when you put your hand to that task, giving yourself in the accomplishment of it. God's peace is upward, it's inward, and then in natural sequence it's—

Outward.

Harmony with God and peace with oneself will bring harmony between men. There's no other way. The reason our world is a problem world is because we have so many problem people. The problems of the world are but the magnification of the problems of individuals like you and me. To get peace in our world we've got to get peace into the hearts of men. Now if this peace comes from God, if Jesus Christ is the One who has made this peace, then Christ must come into the hearts of men before we will have real peace.

That crude cross on which Christ died has become the symbol of peace. Two pieces of wood reach in different directions. One piece points from God to man and man to God and the other piece of wood reaches out from man to man to include all humanity. When will we understand that God's peace is a Person, not a thing! It can't be bought, it can't be achieved by education; it comes when we receive a Person. Apart from the person of Christ there can be no real peace between men.

When we reject Jesus Christ, we declare war on God and friends, and that's a battle man cannot win. Man's arms are too short to fight with God, but God's arms are not shortened that he cannot save all who come to him through Christ. I like J. B. Phillips' translation of Ephesians 2:16. "Then he [that is, Christ] came and told both you who were far from God and us who were near that the war was over." I like that. Jesus came to tell man the war is over. First-century Christians knew that their faith was real when the racial hostility between Jew and Gentile was obliterated and merged into the fellowship of the Christian gospel. They knew that a change had taken place when they loved those they once hated. That's the test, isn't it? The test is in this outward relationship between ourselves and our fellowman. You may know your faith is real when you walk in the Spirit, when you lay down your guns and quit fighting, when you accept God's way for your life and pray for grace to be faithful walking therein.

The sacrifices of love, the spontaneity of joy, and the serenity of peace unite in the life of one who walks in the Spirit. Christ in you: love, joy, peace. This harvest will deliver us from the fitful frustrations of hate, despair, and strife, and all of these tragically are in evidence in the lives of many church members. Walking in the Spirit will produce the harvest of God; love, joy, peace. My friends, that's the highway that leads out of human misery, defeat, and despair. "This is the way, walk ye in it."

4.
Christ in You:
Longsuffering

The nine virtues named in this text are proof of the possession of God's Spirit. They are products of his presence. Their absence in the life of a believer makes one question the presence of the Holy Spirit.

We do well to familiarize ourselves with those fruits of the flesh, or the harvest of the flesh, Paul has outlined so explicitly in preceding verses in Galatians. When those are present, they indicate we are walking apart from Christ—not with Christ. The presence of these characteristics leads us to believe the presence of the Holy Spirit is a reality in the life of a believer.

These nine fall into groups of three. The first three, love, joy, and peace are virtues that come from God. The Bible teaches "love is of God." The Bible states "rejoice [or joy] in the Lord." Jesus stated, "My peace give I unto you: not as the world giveth, give I unto you." So love, joy, and peace are virtues that come from God. We can't whip them up. We can't create them by positive thinking. We cannot develop these of ourselves. Love, joy, and peace come from God and from him alone. In Galatians 1:3 Paul wrote, "Grace to you and peace from God." These come only from him. These are not human attributes that we are responsible for producing.

41

The first of the three, love, is the foundation for the other two. Love is the beginning; but then comes joy, which is love exulting; and peace, which is love reposing. This triad is the foundation for the other six.

The second three, longsuffering, gentleness, and goodness are dispositions that relate to other people; that is, to one's neighbor. The first three have to do with our relationship to God. When that relationship has set, when it has jelled, when we're in right relationship to him through faith in Jesus Christ, love, joy, and peace come. As a by-product of those in our relationship to our fellowman, longsuffering, gentleness, and goodness are marks of our walk with Christ. The first three are upward, the second three are outward.

Again, as in the first three, the first of this second triad is the foundation for the other two. Longsuffering comes first. It is built upon by gentleness and goodness. Gentleness is longsuffering in its passive expression; goodness is long-suffering in its active expression. You can see that the apostle Paul, under inspiration of the Holy Spirit, wrote these not in some haphazard way, but like a ladder with each succeeding rung dependent upon the preceding one. Let's note that longsuffering can be seen in a—

Pattern.

The Greek word rendered longsuffering is *makrothumia*. It is a combination of the word *makros* which means long, and *thumas* which means passion. *Makrothumia*, literally translated, is longsuffering or long passion. The word *makros* meaning long or large is often used in English. You also use the word *micro* in English, which is a Greek word and means small. Both of these are used in the jargon of the youth of today. You refer to a skirt that is a micro-mini, which means a very, very short skirt. The word *makros* is used in reference to something that is long or big, and so these words are not unfamiliar to the minds of those who use the English language.

Our pattern for this longsuffering is the patience of God. Oftentimes this word is rendered *patience*. The literal rendering is longsuffering. Through the pages of the Old Testament we find a record of God's longsuffering or patience with human beings. Reference is made to this divine attribute in a verse that tells us a thousand years with God is as but a day, and a day is as a thousand years. So the longsuffering and patience of God can be seen in contrast with man's patience. Man's desire is for something to take place now rather than waiting patiently for it to come to pass.

In our frantic age we often ask, "Why does God allow certain things to happen? Why doesn't God put a stop to war, sickness, hatred, prejudice, bloodshed, murder, and all of the evil we find in human beings in our world? Why doesn't God step in and stop all this?" I don't have the answer, but maybe 2 Peter 3:9 affords us some insight. "The Lord is not slack concerning his promise, as some men count slackness; but is longsuffering to us-ward [that is toward you and me], not willing that any should perish, but that all should come to repentance." Why does God allow war, sickness, cancer, hatred, prejudice, animosity, and all of these other evils to continue unchecked? Because God is longsuffering, and if he were to step in to put a stop to these, who would be left? If God were to wipe out all hatred, how many of us would be here tomorrow morning? If at midnight tonight God would say, "All right, I'm through, this is enough, my patience is exhausted, I'm going to stop it," how many of us would escape divine judgment and wrath? We can thank God he is longsuffering, that he's patient in this regard.

The patience or longsuffering of God is directly connected with his redemptive purpose. He is longsuffering to usward because he is not willing that anyone should perish, but that all should come to repentance. The only reason the return of Christ has been delayed is because of God's yearning for man's salvation. If he were as impatient as we, he would have already wiped us off the face of his earth.

Remember Simon Peter in his relationship to Jesus Christ. We can see this *makrothumia,* the longsuffering of God in Christ, toward Simon. All through the denials, all through his life of misconception regarding the meaning of the gospel, all through that time when Peter was so slow to perceive that God is no respecter of persons, Christ loved him and never removed him from fellowship. That's the pattern. It's the divine pattern and when Christ is in us that mark in our lives will be obvious for the world to see.

That's the pattern, but the pattern is to be lived out in our lives. That means when our friends are guilty of their inconsistencies, their weaknesses and failures, we're not to wash our hands of them. We're not to say emotionally, "I'll just stop having anything to do with them," for if the Holy Spirit is present in us, like Jesus in his relationship to Peter, we must go on loving. This is the way the world can know we really know Jesus Christ. This pattern is

Personal.

Is there a need for this harvest of the Spirit in our lives today? Do we need longsuffering, or am I talking about an unknown quantity no one needs? I believe we would get a universal affirmation regarding our need for this divine characteristic. If you're unconvinced of the impatience of humanity, let the traffic light change from red to green, and count the seconds before the horn of the car behind you blows—impatience! We want what we want right now, and I'm sure there is a measure of this impatience in the life of every human.

It's wonderful to see the enthusiasm and activism of the youth of this generation. Our young people are ready and willing to go anywhere for almost any purpose. But in addition to this excitement and vivaciousness, youth must learn *makrothumia,* patience, longsuffering. No young person will become an adult in a day. No young athlete will become an all-American overnight. No musically inclined youngster will become a master of the piano, the organ, or any musical instrument in a week or a month. As youth grows into maturity, one evidence of it is development of this characteristic, patience or longsuffering.

Many persons go through life failing to measure up to their fullest potential because of a lack of patience. In our impatience we never wait for God to answer prayer. We never tarry for God's blessings to come—we're always in a hurry.

I think this is probably as true of preachers as anyone else. I believe it is a slam on the Christian ministry for the average length of a pastorate in the Southern Baptist Convention to be three years. What sort of ministry can a person perform in three years? There may be situations where a three-year ministry can be highly effective and used of God, but in the main our patience, our willingness to lay a foundation and to build on that foundation over the years for the glory of God is far more apt to pay dividends and reap spiritual blessings. Preachers are notorious for impatience, but we're simply a reflection of the people to whom we preach. All of society is afflicted by this sin. The reality of our happy fellowship with Christ and the depth of our love for him will be revealed by our patience or our longsuffering.

Paul wrote in that beautiful love poem recorded in 1 Corinthians 13, "Love suffers long." That's a literal translation of this characteristic which is under discussion. Love suffereth long! How many homes could have been salvaged if this Christian characteristic had been present in the hearts of husband and wife? How many marriages could have been saved? How many difficult situations between loved ones could have been avoided if our hearts had been filled with makrothumia? There's little reason to believe that God's love is in your heart or the Spirit of God is producing fruit in your life if you've not gone beyond that childish stage of repaying hate with hate, bitterness with bitterness, littleness with littleness.

Honestly, how long has it been since you've said, "Well, if that's the way he's going to act, I just won't have anything to do with him"? Now how much have you grown with that sort of attitude? Isn't that the most childish of attitudes? What have you done if you just love those who love you? Jesus asked that question, and it's pertinent today (Matt. 5:46). You haven't done anything if the only people you love are those that love you in return. That's like our children. I suppose all children have said as they were growing up, "I'll love you if you'll love me back. If you really love me, you'll do this." That's really not the Christian faith, that's a worldly walk. That's the way the devil's crowd acts. They're happy to love those who love them, but the Christian religion requires that we love the unlovely, because that's the way God loves us and we're unlovely. Yet he loves us nevertheless. If all we're doing is reciprocating in kind, there's a real question as to whether or not the Holy Spirit is present in our lives.

Any fool can answer a fool according to his folly, but it takes a wise man to overcome evil with good, to love them that hate, and to do good to those that despitefully use you. This is a mark of the presence of the Spirit and when he's present, he'll produce this mark.

It takes two to make a fuss. One living under the direction and influence of the Holy Spirit will not be one of such a pair. You're not going to be one of those making a fuss if you're living under God's Spirit and power. This virtue, which is shown to us in a pattern and which becomes personal is also

Persistent.

Love suffereth long, for love never faileth. The father of John Wesley once asked his wife, "How do you have the patience to tell that blockhead boy the same thing 20 times over?" Susannah Wesley with a spirit so like that of Jesus replied, "If I had told him but nineteen times, I should have lost all my labor."

Someone said that diamonds are nothing more than chunks of coal that stuck to their job. Another suggested that most people show more persistency in their first twelve months than they show in their next twelve years, for if they did not, they never would have learned to walk. These are descriptions of the persistency that ought to accompany the longsuffering of Christ in our lives. This is something that keeps on, and on, and on.

The writer of 1 Maccabees said that it was by *makrothu-*

mia that the Romans became masters of the world. How could longsuffering make Rome the mistress of the world? He went on to explain that this Roman persistence would never make peace with an enemy, even though the Romans were defeated. Longsuffering—even in the midst of defeat the Romans wouldn't quit. They kept on until finally the victory came.

Chrysostom called longsuffering the grace that belongs to a man who had the power to avenge himself but who would not. I like that. That's the wisdom of the ages. It is the characteristic of a man who has the power to take revenge but refuses to do so.

Longsuffering is a combination of both courage and patience. Courage and patience unite and hold out, they never give up. This godly virtue is a mark of the presence of the Holy Spirit in our lives. Are you patient and longsuffering?

When the famous artist Leonardo da Vinci was painting his *Last Supper,* he was chided for standing hours at a time before his canvas never making a stroke. Someone asked, "Why do you do this?" His reply was, "When I pause the longest, I make the most telling strokes with my brush."

This characteristic of God, his longsuffering, moved the blind and blessed George Matheson to sing, "O Love that wilt not let me go, I rest my weary soul in thee; I give thee back the life I owe, That in thine ocean depth its flow May richer, fuller be."

It is the patience of God that permits us continued existence, breathing his air, occupying space on the face of his earth. It's his hope that we'll become involved in his program of redemption for all mankind, for God "is not willing that any should perish, but that all should come to repentance."

5.
Christ in You:
Kindness

The King James translation renders this word "gentleness." It's the Greek word *chrestotes*, translated by Thayer in the standard Greek English dictionary as moral goodness, integrity, and kindness. That is the word under discussion now. It's that which Paul has said is the harvest of the Holy Spirit in the life of a believer. If Christ lives in you, this will be the result of his abiding presence. This was an obvious mark of first-century Christians, and has been a characteristic of believers from that day till this.

It was about this kind of Christianity—the Christianity marked by kindness, moral integrity, and goodness—that Tertullian wrote his famous words at the beginning of the third century. He said, "The more we are mowed down in number, the more we grow. The blood of Christians is seed." From the time of Tertullian that statement has been repeated again and again. It seems that when Christians are under the most severe persecution, they multiply the most rapidly. It's when times are hardest Christians are at their best. I believe one reason for this is the presence of the Holy Spirit who leads the Christian into a life of kindness. Christians are kind because the Christ who lives within us is kind. We naturally become like the One we serve. If we are worshiping the true and living God who revealed himself

49

in Jesus Christ, our worship will lead us to likeness. We'll
be like him. Let's begin by having this word *kindness*—

Clarified.

This Greek word is found a number of times in the New
Testament. In four of the places where it appears it is rendered "goodness." In four other places it is translated "kindness" and one time "gentleness."

It has reference to an active, demonstrative kindness. This
is not a passive thing. We considered longsuffering in the
last chapter. Longsuffering takes it and takes it some more.
Longsuffering puts up with evil again and again and again.
Longsuffering is passive in the sense that it does not expect
response. It is characteristic of the life of an individual
because of his inner fortitude.

Longsuffering is not to be confused with kindness. Kindness speaks of a desire for the welfare even of those who
tax our patience. Wouldn't our homes be transformed if they
were marked by kindness? Wouldn't our relationship to
others in the family circle be markedly different if charac-
terized by kindness? Oftentimes we hear of the bad attitude
brothers have for brothers, sisters for sisters, and between
parents and children. Sometimes there is no harmony or
unity within a family circle. The problems of that kind could
be eliminated once and for all if, by the presence of the
Holy Spirit, we became like Jesus in our kindness toward
one another. One translation of the New Testament renders
this word "sweetness." I don't think that's necessarily a sissy
or effeminate word. Sweetness. It has to do with an active
relationship with other people.

This same word, *chrestotes,* is found in Matthew 11:29-30
in describing the yoke of Jesus Christ in the life of the

believer. "Take my yoke upon you," Christ said, "for my yoke is easy." It is the same word and is probably better rendered "kind." Christ's yoke in the life of a believer is kind. That means it does not irk or gall or chafe. It's really the best way of life. That which Christ has to offer us is not something distasteful, evil, and bad; it's not something that will rob us of joy, for his yoke is kind. It's easy to wear because it fits.

A famous rabbi once suggested that kindness is the inability to remain at ease in the presence of a person who is ill at ease. I like that. In fact this same rabbi gave three apt descriptions of kindness. He also said, "It's the inability to have peace of mind when one's neighbor is troubled." Isn't that powerful? All of this is but a description of Jesus, for Jesus was kind.

I think we must face the fact that this kindness is not the product of one's natural inclination. We're not bent toward kindness. We're not naturally inclined to be that way. Our natural inclination is to have our guard up, to fight back and scrap with anyone looking for a fight. That's not the spirit or attitude of Jesus. Though this is not the product of our natural inclination, it is the harvest of the Holy Spirit within us. If we have difficulty at this point, if there is no evident kindness in our lives toward other human beings, we must look to the rock from whence we were hewn, because it speaks of the absence of the Holy Spirit in us.

I remember an act of kindness that impressed me. It was when we were on a trip in 1968 to the Middle East. Everywhere the bus stopped little Arab children would gather around it the moment the brakes brought it to a full stop. Sometimes there would be ten or fifteen standing around, all of them begging. My tendency was to be a little calloused and ignore them. I noticed another preacher in our traveling group, who when he got off the bus, invariably would reach out and put his arm around one of those little Arab youngsters and draw him up close to himself. They were as dirty as children could ever get. There was no evidence that they had taken baths for days or even weeks. There was an odor about many of them, but this preacher invariably put his arm around one of those little dirty, ragged beggars and brought him up close and smiled at him. They could not communicate. They didn't know the English language, and those of us who were on the bus could not speak their language. But you know, that deed of kindness spoke far more eloquently than words. It spoke of love and concern. Isn't that a beautiful picture of Jesus who said, "Suffer the little children to come unto me, and forbid them not: for of such is the kingdom of God."

We would do well to remember that in our relationship to little children and those who tax our patience. We can reveal our Christlikeness just by being kind. It's easy to be abrupt, to cut people off, to be short with them, especially those whose looks we don't like. If they happen to dress differently, if they happen to have a different ethnic background, we might just mark them off rather than being kind to them. This kindness is a characteristic of the presence of God's Spirit in our lives. Having seen it clarified, let's observe kindness as

Character.

In some ways this attribute is similar to longsuffering. It finds its chief object in the evil and unthankful. We're not told to be kind only to those who respond. Our obligation as Christians is to be kind. That means to all people, even those who are not thankful.

While longsuffering is passive and self-contained, kindness is active and busy, doing the Master's business day after day. It is a revelation of character that is completely opposite to the works of the flesh which we find in Galatians 5:19-21. Kindness stands at the opposite end of the spectrum with those works of evil that are evidences of the presence of the devil. The works of the flesh are marked by hatred, wrath, strife, envyings, and things of that kind, all of which are in contrast to our likeness of Jesus Christ and the kindness he brings to the believer.

This character is rather beautifully described in Colossians 3:12-14. There the apostle Paul lists seven garments worn by the Christian, that is, marks by which the world can know that we really do know Jesus Christ. All seven of these garments (the clothing of the child of God) are to be kept in place by a belt of love. Remember those characteristics in Colossians 3, and you can see again the contrast with the works of the flesh. To understand this kindness, it is necessary for us to understand something of the nature and character of God.

God is kind. For a moment let's picture God in human terms as a plutocrat or philanthropist. The word *plutocrat* is the combination of two Greek words, *plutos* and *cratos*. *Plutos* means wealth and authority. This is in contrast to the word *democrat* or *democracy*, because this word is also a combination of Greek words, the word *demos* means people and *cratos*, authority. So a democracy is the rule of the people. A plutocrat is a person who rules by authority because he is wealthy. God is the world's greatest plutocrat from the standpoint of his wealth and authority. He is kind in giving us his finest and best gifts. He's the One who dispenses the riches of his wealth through his kindness toward us. What could be more kind than for God, on the basis of his sacrifice in Jesus Christ, to let us become acceptable unto him, to draw us into the warmth of his fellowship, and give us daily the blessing of his direction and his power?

Our response to the kindness God the plutocrat has shown toward us is the difference between our past in sin and our present walk in Christ. Now, if we're not really saved, our present walk as a church member still reveals the characteristics of the flesh. But if we've been saved, if Christ lives in us through the Holy Spirit, then everything we are and do contrasts with our previous life in sin when we were condemned before God and unrepentant. Kindness must be what we are, but it must also be what we do. See it then as

Conduct.

It is character, but it is also conduct. Who among us could not use a large measure of kindness? This is the opposite to being harsh, bitter, critical, and unkind. I've lived for a number of years in the midst of the hard, cold realities of the business world composed of adults. I've seen all of the meanness and littleness and jockeying for position that takes place in the business world. I've seen businessmen elbow one another out of the way financially and otherwise, and I'm familiar with what takes place in the business community.

I've seen a lot of rascality and unethical acts. I've observed it and so have you, yet I've come to believe that the actions of adults are being equalled by the savage cruelty of young people and teenagers toward one another. Their remarks can be slashing, cutting, and unkind. Young people have become adept at cutting each other and shredding the world to ribbons by their criticism. Who can more quickly hurt another than a young person who freezes out another young person by his attitude and snide comments.

I remind you this can happen as easily in a Sunday School class as on a school campus. Those who go to one high school can be mean, little, and cutting toward those who go to a different high school. That disposition or attitude can spill over into the life of the church if we're not careful. This same ungodly spirit is sometimes reflected in parents. Parents may think more of the schools and school spirit and the relationship between them than they ought to think.

It's easy to be unkind. In our unkindness we should be very careful about driving others away from the kingdom of God. If our lives are what Christ would be in us, our kindness will be as a magnet to attract others. Even those whose skin is a different color, or who attend a different school, or whose economic status is far below our own; all these things will make no difference if Christ lives out a life of kindness in us.

An old proverb suggests that one can pay back the loan of gold, but one dies forever in the debt of those who have been kind. How do you suppose Joseph of Arimathea and Nicodemus felt on the occasion of carrying the body of Jesus from Calvary through the garden into the grave? I wonder if Joseph or Nicodemus felt remorse or regret. As they took the battered, broken body of our Lord, I'm confident they must have remembered the lost years when they knew the truth, and though they believed in Christ, failed to openly confess him. Their devotion to our Lord after he was dead was a beautiful thing. But a clean linen cloth and sweet smelling spices, even added to a costly sepulcher, are no substitutes for devotion and service to the living.

I'm saying show your kindness to the living, not to the dead. I don't think it's nearly so important to take flowers to the cemetery as it is to pass flowers verbally and otherwise to those who are alive. Much bread that has been cast upon the waters has returned buttered, covered with jam, wrapped in wax paper and marked "with love." In your kindness you can cast your bread upon the waters, and if you do it in the Spirit of Jesus, there'll be rewards like you have never imagined.

6.
Christ in You:
Goodness

The Greek word for goodness is *agathosune*. It's a combination of words which mean good. It appears in a number of different places in the New Testament. It was a favorite word of the apostle Paul. He used it in 2 Thessalonians 1:11 and following in his prayer for the young church. He prayed that God's power would satisfy their every desire for goodness. What a beautiful prayer that is: "May the power of God satisfy your every desire for goodness."

Again in Ephesians 5:9 and Romans 15:13 f. this word appears, for Paul used it frequently. In the latter verses, beginning in Romans 15:13, Williams' translation points out that goodness in our lives, a result of the presence of the Holy Spirit, bubbles up and abounds "by the power of the Holy Spirit."

Erdman states that this goodness is love in action. It not only desires the welfare of others but secures the welfare of others. It goes beyond mere benevolence and becomes beneficent. We discover this goodness in a number of ways. Let's look first at the goodness of God, revealed in his—

Works.

One of the most familiar and at the same time one of the most abused verses in Holy Writ is Romans 8:28. Many times we have quoted it and then commented, "Well, I know all things work together for good." This is an inaccurate translation of that verse, for it needs to be understood literally. This verse really states that "GOD WORKS all things together for good to those who love him, who are the called according to his purpose." That simply says that a pagan or infidel cannot claim this promise. It's for those who love God and have responded to his call. The individual who does not know God revealed in Jesus Christ cannot claim Romans 8:28 for himself. "God works all things together for good to those who love him, who are the called according to his purpose."

One person can get nothing but discord from a piano while another can get beautiful harmony. I'm one of those who cannot play a piano or organ. I could sit at the piano or organ for the rest of my life and I doubt if I could ever produce beautiful harmony. I have never studied piano or organ, I just don't know anything about it. It's an impossibility for me. But some musicians I know can play to the blessing of all who hear. Great beauty is produced. It is not the blame of the piano that I'm incapable of producing harmony. The piano or organ may be in excellent condition and of the finest quality. Yet I cannot produce beautiful music on an organ. It's not the fault of the organ.

Life is like that. The potential for either discord or harmony is found in every life. When we live our lives in keeping with God's holy will, our lives produce harmony and beauty. When we live these lives of ours selfishly, trying only to advance our own causes, seeking to magnify ourselves and not God, then the inevitable result is discord and ugliness. It's not the fault of God's work in making us in his likeness, it's the fault of those of us who live not according to his will, but our own.

God's work begins in the moment of existence, for every human being born on earth comes into being as an individual, separate act of the creative power of Almighty God. But God's works don't stop there. God's works are consummated in salvation. What do I mean by salvation? Do I mean only that moment when one comes to say, "I have accepted Jesus Christ as my Savior?" No.

New Testament salvation is threefold. In theological terms, it includes regeneration, sanctification, and glorification. All three of these are component parts and essential to the New Testament experience called redemption. It involves the new birth or regeneration, it involves a life of growing in likeness of Christ or sanctification, and it involves the ultimate experience when we are translated from this life into the presence of our Lord to be his in fellowship eternally unbroken, which is glorification. If you omit any one of these, New Testament salvation does not exist. For instance, if you eliminate regeneration, there is no way to have New Testament salvation. Regardless of how good a person may grow to be, regardless of his hope of eternity, if regeneration has not been experienced—no salvation. If sanctification is absent, that indicates regeneration is missing, for if regeneration has taken place, this involves the implantation of the seed of the Holy Spirit in the life of a believer. He's the One who encourages us in Christlikeness. His presence will mean Christian growth, and the harvest of the Spirit includes these virtues or characteristics under consideration. New Testament salvation finds its consummation in glorification, and if any one of these three is left out, it is not God's plan for redeeming mankind.

This is God's work and in his work we can see his goodness. His work is making us, creating us, placing us here, giving us life, and then offering us his "so great salvation." We also see the goodness of God revealed in his

Will.

God's will is what is best for us. It is encouraging that there are young people who come to believe this and commit their lives in keeping with that conviction. God's will is what's best for you. You may choose an alternative. You may reject God's plan. You may decide to go it alone, on your own, but whatever you choose is second best. God's will is best.

When we come to grips with this truth, then we lay down our arms and run up the white flag of total surrender. As long as we think we know best, the warfare continues and we think God is some kind of intruder trying to force his way into our lives.

Many persons are outwardly respectable but do not possess the inner peace and character that comes as the harvest of the Spirit. This is the reason a person can live an upright life, pay his debts on time, fulfill his responsibilities as a good citizen, provide admirably for his family, be totally acceptable in the eyes of the community, yet die and go to hell. Why? Because respectability doesn't bring salvation. Salvation doesn't come because you pay your debts or live a good life. Salvation comes through Jesus Christ. If you can be saved in some other way, then Jesus died in vain, and he was in error when he stated, "No man cometh unto the Father, but by me."

Persons who live outwardly respectable lives without having had an inner transformation remind me of some pecans I have seen. Often there's a fine, healthy-looking shell, but when you crack it open there's nothing on the inside except a dry, shrunken vestige of what ought to be. Neither the shell nor the insides are of any value. So it is with the life of an individual who tries to be acceptable to God on the basis of his respectability. It's only by the power of God that a human can be fixed up on the inside and made acceptable to God. It's by his will and way that our souls grow and develop. You can have the outer shell of respectability, but if you haven't had the inner transformation you'll never pass God's final examination on the day of judgment.

The Bible teaches that in the day of judgment every person will stand unveiled before the majesty and power of almighty God. This outer shell of body and clothing, possessions and reputation will be once and for all removed. Only the fruit will remain. Only the meat in the shell will exist.

Goodness is a vital aspect of God's will for us. Do you remember the prayer a little girl prayed? "Dear Lord, make all the bad people good and all the good people nice." Wouldn't it be wonderful if all the good people were nice? God's people, Christian people, should be "nice" in their attitudes and relationship to one another, "nice" in their deeds to others.

One day an elderly, black preacher was asked his opinion as to what was wrong with the world. His inimitable reply was, "The good ain't able and the able ain't good." You can flower it up with other words, but I believe he put his finger on the sore spot. Recall God's goodness in relation to our

Witness.

We can see how good God is in his works and will, but

he wants to reveal that same kind of goodness through you and me. There's an old story from the Talmud which holds that a great man once told a servant, "Go to the market and buy me something good." After a time the servant returned with a tongue. On another occasion the master told the servant, "Now, go to the market and buy me something bad." Again the servant brought home another tongue. "Why a tongue each time?" asked the master. The servant replied, "Because the tongue may be a source of either good or evil. If it is good, there is nothing better. If it is bad, there is nothing worse."

I would remind us that our goodness is revealed not only by what we do, but by what we say and the way we say it. Isn't it tragic for church members in good standing to have such a poor reputation among the clerks in the business establishments of a city? It's no different today than it was when I was growing up. I can remember, as a boy, working in a grocery store and standing around on occasion with some of the other young men working there. We would see particular persons come in the store and all of us would run pell-mell to the stockroom before we were seen or forced to wait on that person. It's always sad when a person like that is known to be a member of the church in good standing.

I recently heard an address by Mack J. Spears, president of the New Orleans School Board. Dr. Spears, who is an outstanding black educator and known over the state of Louisiana for his wisdom and the direction he is giving to the school board, made this statement which stuck in my memory. "The more I see of Christians, the greater appreciation I have for infidels." I'll tell you, that hits and hurts. He related the experience that was his as he served as president of the congregation of the church in which he held membership. I don't know exactly what the function of the president of a congregation is, but he said it was during the time when a pastor resigned and they began their search for a new one. It was on the basis of that period of eight or nine months and the reaction of various people in the congregation that led him to make that statement. "The more I see of Christians the greater appreciation I have for infidels."

I'm reminding all of us that the world is observing our witness. The goodness of God that is to be revealed in our lives has been defined as "virtue equipped at every point." R. C. Trench, a great New Testament scholar, suggested that Jesus showed goodness when he cleansed the Temple and drove out the money changers who were desecrating it. This implies that goodness can be both kind and strong. Goodness is not a weak, effeminate sort of emotion. It has strength and sinew and character. Goodness is often enhanced by the company we keep.

A young man came on an occasion to Dwight L. Moody, the great evangelist. He said that in his heart he wanted to reform but didn't know how to give up his undesirable companions. The answer of Dwight L. Moody was a classic. It's as valid today as it was when he said it. He said, "You really do not have a difficult problem. For if you live a life of goodness, your undesirable companions will give you up." You don't have to give up your associates! You live the kind of life Jesus would live if he wore your flesh and your undesirable companions will fade and be gone once and for all. They will not continue their association in the presence of righteousness and morality. They'll do one of two things: They'll either get saved themselves or go their separate ways.

Pride can always be considered a lie. Any evidence of pride in your life or mine is a lie. Any evidence of humility in our lives can always be considered true. Pride makes us think we're something when we're nothing, but humility makes us know we're nothing, and we confess it when we're humble.

Absolute good can only be found in God. On the other hand there is a relative human goodness that can abide in the life of every believer who walks in the Spirit. This is both a challenge and an opportunity. This is one way we have of revealing the abiding presence of the living Christ in our lives. The harvest of the Spirit is goodness. Christ in you will be revealed in this way.

7.
Christ in You: Fidelity

The Greek word found here is the word *pistis*, ordinarily translated faith. It is translated faith when it refers to Christ or God the Father. Usually it is associated with this relationship. But in the construction found in Galatians 5, this word stands alone. It's not used in reference either to the Father, the Son, or the Holy Spirit. It simply stands as one characteristic of those whose lives are Spirit-filled or Spirit-empowered.

In this series of human virtues that are the "harvest" of the presence of the Holy Spirit, this word lends itself to a translation other than "faith." Thayer, who has written the standard Greek-English lexicon used by Greek scholars around the world, suggests that in this particular usage the word refers to "the character of one who can be relied upon." That's far more closely associated with our word *fidelity* than faith.

"The character of one who can be relied on." I suppose that conservatively there is enough preaching in this concept to last a preacher a month or six weeks. One of the glaring weaknesses of humanity today is our inconsistency. We simply cannot be relied upon; we cannot be trusted. Some commentators suggest that we ought to translate *pistis* in this construction, "trustworthiness."

But however we translate it, let's remember that it is descriptive of that virtue which insures obedience to God and loyalty to other people. It is that characteristic which causes one to be true to his promise and faithful to his task. Now in that light, I believe fidelity far more nearly translates *pistis* than faith. Keep in mind then that these nine virtues, falling naturally into categories of three, nevertheless constitute one fruit, singular. Our text does not say, "the fruits" of the Holy Spirit are, but the fruit of the Holy Spirit is. These are not separate characteristics that we work on and develop, that we focus upon and try to build in our lives. These are the inevitable result of the presence of God's Spirit. It's not something then that we do, it rather is something we are. If we are Spirit-filled, Spirit-empowered, Spirit-led, this is the result. All of these characteristics will be inevitable.

The first three of these nine have to do with our upward relationship, with our relationship with God: love, joy, and peace. These can never be apart from a right relationship with the Father God who revealed himself in Jesus Christ. The next three, comprising the second group, including longsuffering, kindness, and goodness, are on a horizontal plane and have to do with our relationship with our fellow-man. We're longsuffering toward those about us. We are kind and good in relation to those with whom we're associated. The last three, of which ours now is number one, include fidelity, meekness, and temperance, or perhaps a better word would be self-control. These have to do with the inner relationship. The first three are upward, the next three outward, and the last three inward. Let's begin by observing the fidelity—

Of God.

God's provision for our salvation and sustenance is constant. It doesn't fluctuate, it's not based on the kind of life we live, and whether we're good or bad. It is based upon our openness to him. His love is constant, his salvation is always available. He is utterly and incomparably faithful in saving those who come to him in faith.

Now the salvation God provides is in three tenses. It is past, present, and future. There are three theological terms used to describe this, with which we are vaguely familiar. These are the terms *regeneration, sanctification,* and *glorification.* God's salvation includes all three. To eliminate any one would be to negate God's salvation. It is not true New Testament salvation if any one of these is missing.

The New Testament clearly describes this, for in Paul's writing we find an allusion to this past experience in the Ephesian epistle when he wrote, "For by grace you *have been* saved." That refers to a past experience, that is for most of us. It's the time when we in personal faith opened our hearts and lives to Jesus Christ and invited him in. For the majority of us that is a past experience. It's something that's already happened. There are myriads who have not yet had that experience. But salvation is past tense for the Christian. It occurred at some time in the past. It occurred when we invited Jesus Christ to come in on the basis of our repentance, faith, and the confession of our sins. He responded and completed this act we call regeneration. Sometimes it is referred to as the new birth, sometimes to being born again, or to being saved, or becoming a Christian. However you may describe it, it's a past experience referring to the moment in time when you individually and personally committed your life to Jesus Christ for salvation.

There is also a present tense to New Testament conversion. It is designated by the theological term *sanctification*. The past tense of salvation is a final, irreversible, never-to-be-repeated act. The present tense of salvation is alluded to in the verse that urges, "Keep on working out your salvation." I think that simply means if you're saved, keep on living like it. Don't continue to revert to the old nature, but reveal the new nature that is in Jesus Christ through your disciplined living. This is the process of sanctification, and by it our faith matures and the image of Christ is more perfectly revealed in us. Why is it then, that so many church members are spiritually stagnant? Stagnation sets in either through a misunderstanding of the totality of salvation or a neglect of the process of sanctification. Maybe some folks don't understand this. Maybe they're not familiar enough with the truths of God's Word to know. Maybe some believe that after the initial act of regeneration, there is no more. Such is not the case. New Testament conversion involves all three; past, present, and future. Possibly this is the reason that many parents and grandparents, physically speaking, are still lapping pablum spiritually when they ought to be eating steak. Perhaps this is the reason that some of the older members of churches, who've been members for the longest period of time, still have not progressed beyond the goo-goo, da-da stage. That's a sad thing. It's sad because of the loss involved. When we could be hitting on eight cylinders, we're limping along and hitting on three or four. What a tragedy! We've never grown in grace and the likeness of Christ.

Possibly this is due to the fact that ego and conceit still sit on the throne of life, for the stock answer that comes from people like this is, "I don't want to," or "I don't like that." How sad! No one can measure the thrust of the kingdom of God that has been stymied, that has been lost by this spirit in the lives of those who ought to be growing and saying, "I'd like to try." Many should say, "I've never done it before but if I can do it for the glory of God, let me try it." Yet we sit back, shrug our shoulders, and mumble, "I don't like that." Has this ever been said in regards to Church Training, or Sunday School? If we're growing, we discover growth comes through spiritual exercise. We don't ever reach a plateau of growth where we no longer need to grow. If we do, if we ever flatten out or stop, like a ball rolled up hill, we lose our momentum and begin to fall backward. Spiritual decay and stagnation have set in for many lives through inactivity alone. "But God is faithful," and in it all his power is available to help us to break the strength of selfishness.

Salvation is also in the third tense, that is future. This is what we call glorification. It has to do with that eternal tomorrow when we shall abide in the presence of our blessed Redeemer. God is faithful, for he provides for all of our needs, past, present, and future. The Christian experience ought to be a growing experience until finally, in the end of life, we're translated from this earth into the presence of our Lord to be like him forever and forevermore. Maybe that's why the New Testament writer wrote, "Wherefore he is able to save them to the uttermost that come unto God by him, seeing that he ever liveth to make intercession for them." This is true fidelity, this is the fidelity of God: ever liveth, maketh intercession. Never will there be a time when it will cease, never a time when his love will be withdrawn from us. This is based on the fact that Jesus said, as a part of his nature, "Him that cometh to me I will in no wise cast out." This is the fidelity of God and the pattern after which our fidelity is to be likened. But turning from the fidelity of God, let's think of fidelity—

In growth.

Our Master stated an unchanging maxim of the faith when he said a tree is known by its fruit. That's one of the most frightening thoughts the human mind can entertain. A tree, which in this instance is a life, is known by the fruit it produces. All of us are trees, and the world knows us by the kind of fruit we bear. What does the world think of us? What is the attitude of others toward us? I mean what we know deep down in our hearts. Not what we try to close our eyes to, not what we try to shrug off with a flippant attitude, but what's the attitude of the world toward us? Do they know that we're little, bitter, complaining, negative people? Or do they know us to be growing, expansive Christians who are trying every day to be more like the Master? We have an obligation to grow in likeness of the Lord Jesus.

P. T. Forsyth, a great conservative theologian of another generation, wrote this immortal statement: "Unless there is within us that which is above us, we shall soon yield to that which is about us." He's saying very plainly that unless the Christian has inner resources, resources that are constantly being replenished, the capacity continually being expanded, unless there is within us that which is above us, we'll soon yield to that which is about us.

It's unfortunate that in the verse division of our King James translation this virtue, *pistis* or fidelity, appeared in verse 22 as if it were a part of the preceding group of virtues.

It's not a fourth member of the preceding group; it's the first of the final group. Perhaps that would be acceptable if this virtue implied trustworthiness, for then it would have reference to man's relationship to man on a horizontal basis. If it referred to the fact that men could trust us, then it could fall into the preceding group. That's not the reference in my opinion, for in the sense in which this word appears in the original language it's not passive but active and requires a different connotation. This is a Christian virtue, not saving faith. Our fidelity and trustworthiness refer to God, his Word, and his will. This is an inner commitment that speaks of our relationship to the Lord.

Fidelity—the quality in one who can be trusted to carry out the responsibilities committed to his hands. The two key words in our fidelity and this process of Christian growth or sanctification are the words *stewardship* and *service*. That's the summation of sanctification: stewardship and service. In the New Testament a steward is one trusted with the keys to his Master's house. The primary requisite of a steward, according to the writings of Paul, is that he be found faithful. All this fits into this characteristic of the presence of God's Spirit in our lives. You see, the Master has no use for stewards who cannot be trusted. This involves our material possessions, but more than that, it involves all we have and are. It involves our personalities in the transmission of the gospel to those who have not heard.

According to 1 Corinthians 4:1 we are stewards of the mysteries of God. That means there is placed upon our shoulders the responsibility of sharing what we know to be true about our Lord. We are stewards of the mysteries of the gospel. You are, I am. I cannot be paid to be your steward, you cannot be bribed into being mine. Each has an obligation to Jesus Christ. You are a steward of the gospel. An unfaithful person, one who is opposite from this characteristic stated in our text, is an undisciplined person. An undisciplined person is an immature person. Many of us have never outgrown the spiritual adolescence that is a part of our initial commitment to Christ. It's based on a lack of understanding, or a lack of knowledge, or on a partial commitment. As we grow, our commitment should grow. Our understanding should grow. The disciplines we apply in our lives ought to become more and more exacting.

We're committed to a revelation of Jesus Christ in us and through us. Some church members remain spiritual pygmies all their lives because of their unwillingness to deny themselves and buckle down to a program of spiritual growth. You don't measure spiritual growth by the number of Sundays you've been out in a year's time. That may refer to a lack of growth. You don't measure Christian growth by the number of trips you've made, or the miles you travel on the weekend. Christian growth is measured by something far different from that. You don't measure Christian growth by the size of the string of fish you catch on a given Sunday, or the number of birdies you made in that golf game. Christian growth is far more likely to be measured by the times that you "stayed by the stuff" and gave yourself to the disciplines of Christian service. It means seeing an opportunity, taking advantage of it, and using what you have for Christ. It means trying to be all Christ would be if he were given that open door of service. We have a responsibility in growth, for when the Holy Spirit is present within us we're committed, and our commitment will be marked by fidelity. One other word. The result of fidelity is

For glory.

This is not self-glorification, it's for the glory of God. That's why we serve! The psalmist David put it in a beautiful way in that very familiar twenty-third Psalm: "He leadeth me in paths of righteousness for his name's sake." Why does Christ lead you through his Holy Spirit? He leads you so he might be magnified and men everywhere might come to know who he is and what he offers. That's why the doors of opportunity and service swing open for us. The Holy Spirit opens those opportunities. I'm talking about the everyday, mundane things. I'm talking about accepting a teaching responsibility with a crowd of juniors who are as active as worms in hot ashes. I'm talking about taking that staid, decaying, dying adult class in which there has not been a new member in years. That's the sort of thing I'm talking about. When the Holy Spirit opens that door for you, what are you to do? By the grace of God, accept the responsibility and fill it for the glory of Christ, for his name's sake!

More and more we hear the excuse, "I'm too busy," or "I'm not going to be here every Sunday." I can understand people being gone some, but I can't understand people being gone every other week, two times every month. For what? What's the reason? Is it an excuse for a lack of spiritual growth? Is that the big thing to which you point as the excuse for your failure to grow in likeness of Christ?

Opportunities abound. The privilege of service is offered, and it's up to us to discipline ourselves and do some things we may not like in the beginning, but which we know we ought to do for our spiritual growth and the glory of our Lord.

Paul suggested in Galatians 6:10 that we are to do good especially for the benefit of "the household of the faith." In the Greek he didn't say household of faith, he said household of the faith. There isn't but one: that's the Christian church! The result of that kind of program is going to be the building of the church, and the heaping of glory on the name of our Lord.

That's why I have a holy distrust of all of these peripheral movements, these superficial groups that are meeting who have no anchor in the body of Christ or the household of the faith. They won't last very long, and there'll be many deceived thereby. Any movement that's going somewhere had better be connected to Christ's church, about which he said: "The gates of hell shall not prevail against it." Sometimes we suffer from the delusion that Christ's church is just an association of human beings brought together by similar humanitarian ideals. That's why some churches are dying. If that's all they've got going, they ought to die and come out from under the banner of Christ.

We're not here simply for humanitarian purposes. We're not gathered here as a body of believers just because of certain similar human sympathies. That sort of teaching and belief is blatant blasphemy. The church is a fellowship of the faith. That faith is based on certain unique facts, and is centered in a certain divine Person. Anything that claims to be a church which isn't based on those facts and centered in Jesus Christ has no right to claim the name.

We're to do good to all men, but especially to those of the household of the faith. That fidelity which is a fruit of the presence of God's Spirit in us reveals itself in our relationship to Christ's church. Don't forget that. I believe it's vitally important.

In 1924 George Leigh Mallory and some other Englishmen attempted to climb Mount Everest. They finally reached 25,000 feet and established a base camp. From there they set out for the summit, but those of the party who tried failed in their quest. Today Mallory and Irving lie buried under the eternal snows of that Himalayan peak. The others in the party returned to England to tell their story. One of these addressed a large audience in London. He had behind him a screen on which was an enlarged picture of Mount Everest itself. As he concluded his speech he turned and addressed the mountain, "Everest," he said, "we tried to conquer you once, but you overpowered us. We tried a second time but you were too much for us." And then he said, "But I want you to know we are going to conquer you, because you can't grow any bigger and we can." Thus, the Christian faces life. Our problems remain but he giveth more grace and we grow stronger through fidelity, through the presence of his Spirit, and we can bring glory to his name.

8.
Christ in You: Meekness

For many church members the Christian life is like a yo-yo. It's a series of ups and downs, and unfortunately for most of us, we're down far more than we're up. When we find ourselves down spiritually and emotionally, the accompanying discouragement makes us think that the Christian life is an impossibility. When we get discouraged, we usually fall by the wayside. When we need Christ the most, we come to him the most infrequently. The person who really needs the ministry of the church in this day is not ordinarily the person who seeks us out. He's the person we must seek out. If this person is a Christian and in a backslidden condition, he has come to feel that there is no hope for him in his particular situation. He needs a Christian to tell him there is hope, that there is an opportunity for him, that there is something he has missed.

We have failed to distinguish the difference between peace with God and the peace of God. There is a tremendous difference between saving faith and satisfying faith. I know many Christians who possess saving faith but who've never found the joy, the lift, the lilt of satisfying faith.

There's a difference between receiving and walking. Paul said it in Colossians 2:6: "As ye have therefore received Christ Jesus the Lord, so walk ye in him." The Christian faith involves receiving and walking. There's a difference between being in Christ and having Christ as Lord in you. And frankly, that's the difference between saving faith and satisfying faith.

Jack Taylor wrote a book that has received a great deal of publicity. We bought the book before leaving on vacation, and I had the privilege of reading it while gone. He used an illustration that stuck in my mind and I think it applies at this point.

Take a cup of water and a tea bag. They are not identical. The cup of water and the tea bag are not synonymous, they're distinct. Heat the water and place the tea bag in it. When this is done, a phenomenon takes place. The water changes both its color and its nature. It is infused by a new and dominant nature. The change continues and is obvious to the eye until that which was water becomes tea. The water no longer exists. It has become a new substance. Maybe the water could say, "It is no longer I that lives, but tea that lives in me."

That's what our text is about. It has to do with Christ in you, which is the hope of glory. Christ in us is that power by which our natures are changed, by which we're no longer what we used to be but are new creatures with an entirely new life, new spirit, and new disposition. Everything about us has changed. "It's no longer I that lives, but Christ who lives in me." Let's begin with an—

Explanation.

We remind ourselves that true meekness is not to be construed as weakness. This virtue, along with love, is distinctively Christian. There's no other religion based on love and meekness. The Greek word translated meekness is *praotes*.

It's a difficult word to translate into English. There's no one word that really embodies everything found in this Greek word.

Thayer's Greek-English lexicon gives us three ways in which *praotes* is used in the New Testament. I think all three are summed up in it. Let's get this. First of all, this word means submission to the will of God. In Matthew's Gospel alone *praotes* is used three times in this sense. To the meek is given the promise to inherit the earth. "Blessed [or happy] are the meek, for they shall inherit the earth." So it means submission to the will of God.

Secondly, it means to be teachable. This is the one who is not too proud or too busy to learn. My, can't you see the need for this meekness today! How many church members are there who think they already have a good grasp on the faith and there's not much else to learn? How many are there who are not enrolled in Sunday School and who never give themselves to training in order to serve Christ better? This word, which is part of the harvest of the Spirit, or what the Spirit of Christ produces in us, means to be submissive to the will of God. It means to be teachable.

Thirdly, Thayer says it means to be considerate. When *praotes* is used in the adjectival sense, it refers to an animal that has been tamed and brought under control. That says something to you and me in our Christian pilgrimage.

We understand that meekness as a virtue in our lives refers to the Christ-mastery of life. It means Jesus is in control. It means we're submissive, we're teachable, and friend, it means we're considerate. Now I could preach for a month or six weeks on consideration. How inconsiderate most of us are. Much of the time our inconsideration focuses in the lives of those we love best. We're just inconsiderate, but true meekness brings a consideration of the needs and for the feelings of other people.

When we use the word *meek*, we usually qualify it by saying "meek as a lamb." Or maybe "meek as a mouse." Now that brings to mind a scared, scampering creature that will run if someone says boo! Meekness equals weakness in the minds of most of us. Let's try to rescue this word and attach its true Christian significance. It means a spirit submissive to God. It means a life that is teachable in the things of Christ, and a human who is considerate of his fellowman. That's an explanation of *praotes*. But let's see our—

Example.

It's interesting to recall from the Old Testament it was said of Moses, "The man Moses was very meek, more than all men that were on the face of the earth." Now was Moses weak? Not unless you call a murderer weak. He saw an injustice being done and slew an Egyptian—killed him. He wasn't afraid. He didn't have that kind of meekness. I'm not condoning murder! I'm not saying to you prove your meekness by going out and killing somebody. Not at all. I'm saying that being afraid is not a characteristic of meekness. Meekness has to do with something else.

Yet to find the supreme example of meekness we have to come to the New Testament. Paul, in his second Corinthian correspondence pleaded with the Corinthian Christians, "by the meekness and gentleness of Christ." In Matthew 11:28-30, Jesus said: "I am meek and lowly in heart." In living his life Christ became the example for all men to follow. In giving his life he became man's sacrifice for sin. Meekness, then, becomes a complement to our faith.

It's not a lack of spirit; it's not an incipient cowardice; it's not a retiring disposition. It is a fruit of the presence of the Holy Spirit requiring the highest courage and activity and proves the presence of Christ in the heart of a believer. Submission to the will of God, teachable, considerate of other people.

Jesus Christ had no fear for his personal safety. He wasn't trying to save his own skin or protect his own neck. He didn't have any regard or consideration for public opinion. It didn't make any difference what other people thought of him. The one thing about which he was primarily concerned was submission to the will of God. True meekness ought to center in this. In perfect meekness Jesus Christ lived his life in obedience to God's command and was totally oblivious to the jeers and taunts of his contemporaries. He's our example. Let's think now of the—

Embodiment

—of this characteristic. Four verses following our text, that is Galatians 6:1, we have an indication of how this meekness is to be used. If you have your Bibles open, look at it. "Brethren, if a man be overtaken in a fault, ye which are spiritual, restore such a one in the spirit of meekness." Maybe this verse explains why efforts at church discipline have largely failed. If you go to a sinning brother, a fellow member of the church, in a spirit of pride, that simply leads to more sin. If meekness is found in the heart of the one who goes to a sinning brother, and meekness is found in the heart of the one who has sinned, this will render the former incapable of pride and make the latter teachable.

Assuming the Holy Spirit is present in the lives of both, then there is a redemptive situation. If there's pride in the heart of the one who says, "Look, you're guilty of this, you must stop it and apologize to the church," then immediately the defense of the sinning brother comes up. He's ready to fight.

Obviously, if one in sin is filled and motivated by the Spirit of Christ, he will be willing to admit his error and need for a new and deeper commitment to Christ. If he lacks meekness, this leads to self-satisfaction, arrogance, and conceit. He's likely to say, "I'm as good as any member of that church." This reveals a lack of meekness and the absence of the Holy Spirit. Maybe from a negative standpoint a sinning brother might respond, "Well, I'm no worse than any of the other members up there." Do you know how many times I've heard that? Dozens and dozens and dozens of times. Talk to any lost man! Talk to any indifferent member of the church and the chances are excellent that his attitude will be, "Well, I'm no worse than . . ." This reveals a lack of the Holy Spirit's presence. The person who is Spirit-filled and motivated is not interested in being "no worse than," he's interested in being more like Jesus Christ. He's not comparing his life to the lives of others horizontally. The one filled with the Spirit of Christ is comparing himself with the Lord Jesus on a vertical plane. The harvest of the Spirit is meekness. Where this spirit prevails there is unity and harmony in the things of Christ.

Jesus said, "Come unto me, all ye that labour and are heavy laden, and I will give you rest. Take my yoke upon you, and learn of me: for I am meek and lowly in heart: and ye shall find rest unto your souls." Remember the old-timers talking about soul rest? Old-time preachers used to preach on soul rest. Jesus said in Matthew 11:28-30 that he would give two kinds of rest. "Come unto me, all ye that labour and are heavy laden, and I will give you rest." Then he said if you "Take my yoke upon you, and learn of me . . . ye shall find rest unto your souls."

You get a certain kind of rest through forgiveness, a saving kind of rest, but you don't get that satisfying rest until you take Christ's yoke and begin to learn of him. This is the sweet peace that results from the forgiveness of sin and the joy of serving Christ. It involves the assurance of membership in the family of God, but there is something more. It is the wonderful joy that comes in seeing a need, in feeling the impulse of the Holy Spirit, and moving to meet that need in the Spirit of Christ. The first rest depends upon our coming to Jesus for salvation. The second rest involves taking up the yoke in service.

The yoke is a symbol of submission. It speaks of obedience. Some persons who really do know Jesus Christ as Savior have not yet become submissive to his will and have never found soul rest or a satisfying faith. You can read the Bible through and through, you can study it every day and still find something missing in your life. You can pray at regular periods and for long hours at a time and still find something missing in your life. It's only when you take Christ's yoke that you learn his will.

Jesus said his yoke is easy. Most of us don't think of any yoke that way. We don't like to be told we have to do something. We don't want to be obedient to someone else. But Jesus said, "My yoke is easy," and he meant that it was easy because it fits. Whatever it is Christ has for you to do, that's the best thing for your life. It fits you. He matches the talents and abilities that he has given with the challenge he has in mind for you, and together the two mesh. As you begin to serve him and follow his will, you'll find that satisfying faith. This abiding soul rest enables you to get up every morning and say, "Good morning, Lord, thank you for the night's rest, I'm reporting for duty." You'll find the "peace of God that passeth all understanding."

One thing is certain. Christ cannot harness you or put his yoke on you while you're running. If you're in motion, there's not much he can do to get you harnessed up for the work of his kingdom. If you're willing to be harnessed, it requires the same thing from you that it requires of a horse.

On a recent Saturday afternoon, we went to a nearby ranch. The owner had three horses out in the pasture. We were going to saddle and bridle those horses and ride them. Do you know how we did it? Right! We took some feed and began to drop a little, and then began to feed them by hand and finally got them close enough so the rancher got his arm around the neck of one of the horses and got the bridle in his mouth. But that horse was standing still! We never would have gotten the bridle in his mouth if he'd been running.

God can't put his harness on you or his yoke while you're in motion. I sometimes think that's the reason for many of these senseless, needless, out of town weekend trips. A lot of people I know and you know are running from God, and the best way to do it is to stay out of pocket. Just don't show up except on certain infrequent occasions. When you stop, when you heed the biblical admonition, when you get submissive, when you get willing to take Christ's yoke, then you can find the satisfying faith! You don't have to run somewhere every weekend looking for peace, looking for something new, for a satisfaction you've never had. You can find it right where you are when you take Christ's yoke, get harnessed up, and begin to do what he wants you to do.

The Bible says, "Be still, and know that I am God." You have to put on the brakes, put the car in the garage, turn off the engine long enough for the motor to cool off, and tune in on God. Make yourself available. Now if you're aware that there's a missing quality in your Christian experience, if you know that you've really never let Christ live in you, then slow down! Come to a full stop and allow Christ your Savior to become Christ your Lord. Then you can say with our friends who have these bumper stickers, "Jesus is Lord." It's a way of life, but you can't say it until his yoke has been placed on you.

Meekness is wrapped up in all of this—submission to the will of God, teachableness and consideration for people. "Christ in you," Paul said, "the hope of glory." And if Christ lives in you, meekness will be a part of your demeanor.

9.
Christ in You: Temperance

It's highly doubtful that our word *temperance* conveys to mind the true meaning of the Greek *egkrateia,* which is the word in our text. This word is derived from another Greek word, *kratos,* and the meaning of it is self-control. Actually we don't think of temperance in this light. Temperance for most of us has to do with abstinence from alcoholic beverages, but in the construction of our text the word can mean self-control or the power to take hold of. This literally means that virtue found in the life of one who masters his desires and passions, especially his sensual appetite.

We find this word a number of times in the New Testament. Paul doubtless is thinking in terms of the control of one's entire life under the direction of the will of God. This word then applies to one who has submitted his life to God's direction. It's that sort of self-control. We find this same word, *egkrateia,* in 2 Peter, in Acts, and on two occasions in 1 Corinthians. One of these refers to the control of sex and two refer to the control of self.

The fruit of the Spirit is singular. But the fruit of the Spirit is like a pie that has been divided into segments. Each one of these is required if there is to be a whole. So it is with these nine characteristics of the presence of God's Spirit.

It requires the sum total of all of them in a life committed to Jesus Christ to reveal the presence of Christ. *Egkrateia,* self-control. This ninth segment is a very vital part of the harvest of the Holy Spirit. It has to do with oneself. It's not like the first three that have to do with our relationship to God in a vertical dimension. It's not like the second three that have to do with man's relationship to his fellowman. These last three refer specifically to man's relationship with himself. Let's look at self-control in regard to—

Passion.

I read an interesting story recently of a sixth-grade boy who was writing a school essay on the process of human birth. He went first to his grandmother and asked her about it. She replied that the doctor brings babies in a little black bag. Then he asked his father. He looked over his paper long enough to say the stork brings you. Finally, he asked his oldest sister. She looked at him with a benign smile, and related how the fairy brings you and leaves you under the mulberry bush. He went back to his writing, and after a time went to bed. The curiosity of his father had been aroused, so he went in to see what his son had written. The concluding sentence written by this sixth grader was: "After careful research I must conclude that there has not been a natural childbirth in our family in three generations."

This is approximately the position in which some of us as parents find ourselves today. I'm sure many of you are sympathetic toward it. With remarkable candor, the apostle Paul discusses the problems of sex in 1 Corinthians 7. He talks of how it relates to those who are unmarried, those who are married, those who once were married and now have lost a loved one, or by divorce are living in a single state. All of these areas are covered as the apostle points his finger toward a very vital spot in the life of human beings. Paul uses the word under discussion in our text, the word that we render self-control, stating with stark realism that married people have no right to deny sex relations to one another. He says this is part of our self-control. It's our giving of self to each other within the marriage context.

In one of Homer's Greek mythologies, he tells the story of an island inhabited by beautiful, seductive maidens. Their singing caused many ships to be destroyed on the reefs surrounding the island. Ship captains who were forced to pass that way tried a number of methods to foil the temptation. Some filled the ears of their sailors with wax so they could not hear the songs of the sirens. Ulysses plugged his sailors' ears with wax and lashed himself to the mast of his ship so that he might be kept safe. As he heard the seductive singing he was unable to respond, unable to direct the ship toward the inducement.

Yet Jason and his crew found an even better method. He took on board his ship a man named Orpheus. He was the sweetest singer of his day. When Jason's ship neared the island, Orpheus played his lyre and sang a song far more grand than the cheap, seductive song of the maidens. The songs of the sirens were no match for the sweet singing of Orpheus.

I believe there's an application to be made here in the life of a Christian when it comes to self-control in the matter of passion. A Christian exercises self-control in the arena of sex, not because sex is dirty, but because sex is holy. The reason a Christian does not tell dirty jokes about sex is not because sex is unclean and off limits, but rather because sex is holy and to be fulfilled in the manner God himself prescribed. Because it is a gift of God, it is to be used according to the directions of his holy Word.

We've had a stir in school systems across the land over sex education. My opposition to sex education in the schools centers in the individual who might be teaching my children. I would not want my children to think that this was merely a biological function, for to teach sex from that standpoint is nothing more nor less than subtle blasphemy. This is a gift of God, and can never be fully understood apart from the plan and purpose of God. It can never achieve its beauty until it is interpreted as an act of love between those who are married, for it's in that commitment that there is security, joy, and peace of mind.

The Victorians talked a great deal about love but knew very little about sex. Perhaps it's time that modern Americans, who seem to know a great deal about sex, begin to talk once again about love. Sex out of the context of love is really nothing more really than a biological function. That's not the way God intended it. This is one of the marks that separates Homo sapiens from an animal. This is not just a function of the human body. It's to be an expression of love between two individuals. It's not a relationship that affects no one but me, or no one but you. It's a relationship that always affects two people and most of the time three or more. That's why God in his Word has given us the clear directions as to the use of this holy gift. Paul uses the word *self-control* in regard to our passion but let's see this self-control in regard to our—

Person.

The word appears again in 1 Corinthians 9:24 f. in regard to oneself. There are two illustrations the apostle uses here:

one is running, the other is boxing. Both of these athletic endeavors require self-control, *egkrateia*. This means we must apply self-control in our lives as Christians, understanding that the Christian life is a disciplined life. It's not unbridled or unbuttoned living, it's controlled living that moves us from where we are to a certain known goal. That goal is likeness with Jesus Christ.

Both running and boxing require rigorous training and strict discipline for competition. If you're to compete in any running game, you must train. You must bring yourself under control and get in shape to engage in that kind of competition. The winning runner in Paul's day received a crown of ivy, or maybe pine, but it soon withered, died, and was gone. All those days, weeks, and months of rigorous training were for the receipt of a crown corruptible. Paul takes this and applies it spiritually, pointing out that God's child, the Christian, the follower of Jesus Christ, brings himself under control, exercises personal discipline, not for a corruptible crown such as ivy or pine, but for an incorruptible crown that "fadeth not away." This is the purpose of bringing ourselves under control, putting a bridle in our mouths, bits in our teeth, and saying like Paul, "This one thing I do."

Self-control eliminates the possibility of shadowboxing, or just beating the air. Paul takes this very common figure and concluded that it really does not accomplish much. If all you're doing is shadowboxing, you're not really engaging in this sport. Maybe we see this as an allusion to hypocrisy. The person who is constantly shadowboxing and never engages in a real match against a real opponent does not have much he can say to the rest of us regarding his self-control. It's the man who's been in the ring against an opponent who has something to offer others from experience.

If all you've been doing in your Christian life is shadow-boxing, going through the motions, following a little routine or a pattern, attending church once in a long while, or maybe mouthing some pious shibboleth, you're just shadowboxing. That's the kind of hypocrisy the world is fed up with on the part of Christians. It's that from which the world has turned in utter disgust. What the world wants to know is, are you for real? Is what you have genuine, or are you just telling something you heard somebody else say? Paul called this shadowboxing. Self-control eliminates this possibility.

Through rigorous training and discipline one can prepare himself spiritually to deliver that knockout blow. No one of us will ever do much for the world until first we have done something with ourselves. Show me an undisciplined person and I'll show you one who never contributes to life. An undisciplined person doesn't even contribute to his own family.

This is a great disease that has infected the youth of America. A segment of our young people in America have "copped out," withdrawn from society and developed their own little communes and way of life in which there are no disciplines. They amount to nothing, they contribute nothing to the world. The sad part about it is that sometimes this is identified with the Christian faith. That's a spurious kind of faith, not the faith revealed in the New Testament. Paul says one of the evidences of God's Spirit's presence is self-control. If Christ is in you, you'll lead a disciplined, well-ordered life.

The longer an orchestra plays the more it needs time out to tune up. The farther an airplane flies the more ground service it requires to be put back in shape to fly again. There's no evading that law in any realm of life. This is especially true in the Christian realm, for discipline accompanies a Christ-dominated life.

There are some things a Christ-dominated person will do. I think of the spiritual exercises such as daily prayer, daily Bible study, daily availability for service, faithfulness in the support of the work of the kingdom through Christ's eternal church. These are disciplines that always accompany a Christ-dominated life. This control of self means that we say no to some things that we might like to do, to do some things that we may not like at first but which we know are essential to Christian growth.

The young men of our city and nation engaged in football activities now, if they're honest, would have to admit that they would prefer not to practice. If they could just play in the games and be exempt from all the perspiration and bruises and labor of daily practice, it would be wonderful! But daily practice is a part of the discipline of engaging in this athletic endeavor. So it is in the Christian life. We may not like some of the things Christ expects of us in the beginning, but the more we become like him the more we'll fall in love with these things that lead to spiritual maturity. Now let's apply this principle of self-control in the area of—

Purpose.

I'm speaking not of our purpose, but the purpose or will of God. An old ship captain once said, "I've always lived by the philosophy that if the sea is smooth, it'll get rough, and if it's rough, it'll get smooth. But with a good ship you can always ride it out." That's a good philosophy for life, especially if that life has been submitted to the control of God's Holy Spirit. This then is the ultimate in self-control:

to so completely own ourselves that we can give ourselves to someone else. There is no real self-control until we come to that point. When we've taken ourselves in hand, then we have the capability of giving ourselves to someone or something else. For the Christian, that someone to whom we give ourselves is the Spirit of Christ revealed through the Holy Spirit in directing our daily activities.

The fulfillment of God's purpose in you may seem an insurmountable barrier. Maybe you, like some others, have already discerned what God wants you to do with your life. But immediately self begins to bring up the excuses and barriers. You can see so many reasons why this just isn't plausible. Rather than attacking the problem, you quit the field of battle. You see God's will as the impossible dream.

When mountain climbers see a mountain from a distance, it seems to be huge and unconquerable. But the closer the mountain climber gets to the mountain the more clearly he sees the mountain passes by which that mountain becomes accessible. If they never come closer, they never see the possibility of climbing that mountain. One never comes closer without faith, hope and confidence.

So it is with the will of God. It may seem far too involved and complicated for you. You may not see how you will be able to engage in weekly Bible study and teaching others in a Sunday School class. It may seem that your talents are not such that you're fitted for such a responsibility. But if God is speaking to your heart and directing you to accept, face it with hope, confidence, and faith. The closer you come to it, the more you'll see how God is able to make a way for you.

All this involves controlling ourselves so totally that we can give ourselves into his hands.

Many of you have heard the old parable of two frogs who fell into a container of cream. They tried to leap out, but couldn't make it. One of the frogs was a pessimist. He began to think defeatist thoughts, and the acids of futility spread over him. He finally convinced himself there was no way out and no need to try. In despair and total resignation he sank to his death in the cream.

The other frog was optimistic, possessed by both faith and confidence. He said to himself that he might die in that container of cream, but if he did, he would go down with every flag flying. He swam, thrashed around, beat the cream, and made a great stir. Gradually he began to feel solid footing. His legs, moving like little pistons, got traction, and finally he leaped from the container, the contents of which had now been churned into solid butter!

Self-control is for a purpose. That purpose is to prove the presence of the Holy Spirit in us, and that "in all things Christ might have the preeminence."